Suburban life in Roman *Durnovaria*

Excavations at the former County Hospital Site
Dorchester, Dorset 2000–2001

by Mike Trevarthen

with contributions by
Catherine Barnett (neé Chisham), Kayt Brown, Nicholas Cooke, Stephen R. Cosh,
Brenda Dickinson, Jessica M. Grimm, Sheila Hamilton-Dyer, Jacqueline I. McKinley,
Matt Leivers, J. M. Mills, Jane Sidell, Rachael Seager Smith,
Chris Stevens and Sarah F. Wyles

Illustrations by
Karen Nichols

Published 2008 by Wessex Archaeology Ltd
Registered Office: Portway House, Old Sarum Park, Salisbury SP4 6EB

British Library Cataloguing in Publication Data
A catalogue record for this book is available from the British Library

ISBN 978-1-874350-46-0

Edited by Philippa Bradley and Julie Gardiner
Designed and typeset by Karen Nichols

Printed in the United Kingdom by Henry Ling Limited,
The Dorset Press, Dorchester DT1 1HD

Cover illustrations:
Front: Reconstruction looking south-west across the site during the middle Roman period, by K Nichols.
Contents page: Rare Roman bone hairpin representing Amor, from excavations at Chesil Place (figure height 27mm).
Back: Excavating the late Roman mosaic.

Contents

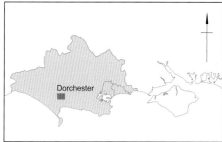

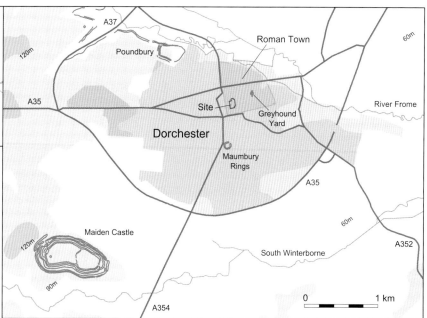

Figure 1: Location of site within the Roman town of Durnovaria and modern Dorchester

Summary

Excavations at the former County Hospital site, Dorchester have provided a rare opportunity to examine a reasonably large area of the south-western corner of the Roman town of *Durnovaria*. This has enabled the development of this part of the Roman town to be established more fully. Evidence for a series of buildings, including a late Roman town house complete with fine mosaics, was recovered. Other structures, working areas and probable barns were also identified. The excavations produced a wealth of artefactual evidence shedding light on the daily lives and activities of the inhabitants of the town. Imported items such as pottery were recovered together with some of the foodstuffs that may also have been brought from the continent. Important evidence for *allec* or fish sauce was recovered; this is the furthest west it has been found in the Roman Empire and one of only a few examples of this foodstuff from Britain. Other possible imported items include wine or vine fruits, olive oil, grain and lentils. Local produce and commodities were also consumed and used within the town including foodstuffs, livestock and regionally produced pottery and items such as shale. The evidence from previous excavations in the vicinity has also been used to set the results into context. The excavations generated immense local interest and the open day proved so popular that many people queued for hours for a glimpse of the beautiful mosaics, buildings and artefacts revealed. With this in mind the results of the excavations are presented here in a less formal manner than is usual for archaeological reports and we have included many photographs and images to allow a broader understanding of the archaeology to be conveyed. Technical reports on aspects of the results (detailed stratigraphic descriptions), the finds and environmental reports will be available on Wessex Archaeology's website. It is hoped that this volume will have a wide appeal to residents of Dorchester, those interested in Roman archaeology and the academic community.

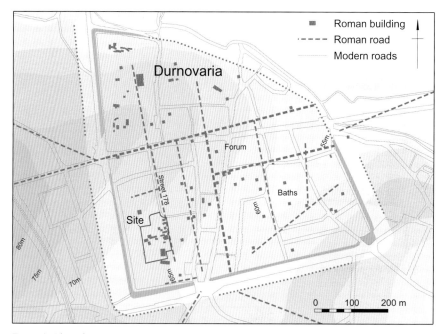

Figure 2: Plan of Roman Durnovaria showing the location of the site

Introduction

Dorchester, the ancient county town of Dorset, has historic roots extending back to at least the 10th century (Fig. 1). In the reign of King *Athelstan* (AD 925–939) it had a market, became a borough (a legally recognised defended settlement), and a mint was established. A royal residence is known from 9th–10th century charters and other documents (Penn 1980, 60). A castle existed by 1137, but was ruinous by the beginning of the 14th century (Penn 1980, 61, 63).

Today the town thrives as a busy commercial and residential centre (Fig. 3): it is the seat of local government for the county, and for West Dorset District, and is internationally renowned as the home of the 19th century novelist and poet Thomas Hardy.

However beneath the centre of modern Dorchester lie the remains of a yet older town, the Roman settlement known as *Durnovaria*, which developed and flourished after the Roman Conquest of Britain (AD 43), remaining an important regional administrative centre until the later 4th–early 5th century. (the term 'Roman' is used here to include Romano-British ie native but Romanised finds and features).

Whilst there have been many archaeological excavations within Dorchester and many more minor works of observation and recording, it is commonly noted that remarkably little is known about the Roman town in terms of the layout of its major public and religious buildings (with the exception of the baths), of the precise positions of its approach roads and town gates, or of its grid of streets.

Opportunities to undertake large-scale archaeological excavations within Roman Dorchester are rare which is why the redevelopment of the former County Hospital site is important (Figs 2–3). A few notable exceptions include the excavations at the Wollaston Field Baths (English Heritage in prep.), Greyhound Yard and Old Methodist Chapel (Woodward *et al.* 1993), and Charles Street (Adam *et al.* 1992; Adam and Butterworth 1993). More recently excavations have been undertaken on the northern part of the former County Hospital site (Cox in prep.) and Dorchester Post Office (Wessex Archaeology 2005).

Figure 3: Aerial view of site showing the redevelopment

Figure 4: Portrait of the architect Benjamin Ferrey (1810-1880)

Benjamin Ferrey F.R.I.B.A. (1810–80)

Benjamin Ferrey (Fig. 4), from Christchurch and educated in Wimborne, became a pupil of the famous Gothic revival architect Augustus Pugin (1769–1832), studying with Pugin's son. He built a large architectural practice in London and became one of the earliest members of the Royal Institute of British Architects. Ferrey was also Diocesan Architect to Bath and Wells and worked with Sir George William Tapps-Gervis to develop the Westover Estate in Bournemouth. As well as the main block of the Dorset County Hospital (Fig. 5), Ferrey designed other Dorchester buildings including All Saints Church (1843–5), the Municipal Buildings (1848), Holy Trinity Church (1875–6) and numbers 4 and 5 High West Street (formerly, Williams' Bank). The Williams family of Bridehead (Little Bredy) became patrons of Ferrey and were also sponsors of the County Hospital. Arthur Acland-Troyte, who became an architect under Ferrey's guidance, assisted him with the design for All Saints Church. He died in 1857 and was commemorated by the Chapel of the Hospital which was completed in 1862.

Construction of the hospital was not completed without problems. An entry in the Minutes of the Hospital Committee (DHC reference NG/HH/DO(c)/1/1/1) dated 26 September 1844, charts one such incident (some modern punctuation has been inserted to make sense of the manuscript text): *'The Eastern main wall after coming four or five feet above the ground level was not properly filled in. Baskets of small stuff were thrown in, baskets of grout were thrown in now and then more than four feet apart. I can put my hand upon parts of the wall where, if the face was taken off, the dry stones would tumble out of the middle. There was neither grout or mortar. It is so generally throughout the walls. All the men that have worked with trowels have said that they never saw work filled in this manner, never saw it done so before, never saw it so bad.'* Later the same entry states: *'I have heard Mr. Goddard tell the men not to use too much mortar. I have heard him abuse the young men for doing so.'*

English Heritage, The Lists of Buildings of Special Architectural And Historic Interest
http://www.communigate.co.uk/dorset/clhs/page13.phtml

Excavations were also undertaken in 1969 and 1970 prior to construction of Hospital wards (Patrick Greene 1993). Important work took place before the Second World War at Colliton Park (Drew and Collingwood Selby 1937; 1938; RCHM(E) 1970). The excavations carried out for Bentleigh Cross Limited at the former County Hospital site in 2000–1, presented here, have added significantly to our understanding of Roman *Durnovaria* and, in particular, have illustrated with uncommon clarity some of the changes it underwent in the 3rd and 4th centuries AD.

Figure 5: Benjamin Ferrey's drawing of the west front of the proposed Dorset County Hopsital (1840)

Regenerating the former County Hospital site

The formal opening of the new Dorset County Hospital at Dorchester by The Queen on 8 May 1998 marked a new chapter in the provision of healthcare for the County. Its inauguration also quietly brought to a close a century-and-a-half long tradition of medical care at Dorchester's 'old' County Hospital. This earlier facility, founded in 1838, had greatly outgrown its origi-nal home, Benjamin Ferrey's imposing hospital building of 1841–46 and, by the later 20th century, had developed into a sprawling and ill-matched com-plex of buildings awkwardly locked within Dorchester's increasingly con-gested historic core. Though most of it is now demolished, among the few remaining buildings are Ferrey's origi-nal hospital building (Grade II listed), and Somerleigh Court, now Edgcumbe Manor, a mid-Victorian town mansion near Alexandra Terrace.

A scheme to regenerate the County Hospital site led to a series of archaeo-logical excavations in autumn 2000–1 (Fig. 6). Redevelopment of the site was substantially completed in 2005–6, and the three new ranges of close care residential and nursing apartments which now flank a south-ern extension to Somerleigh Road were named Chesil Place, Hascombe Court and the Somerleigh Court Nursing Home (Fig. 6).

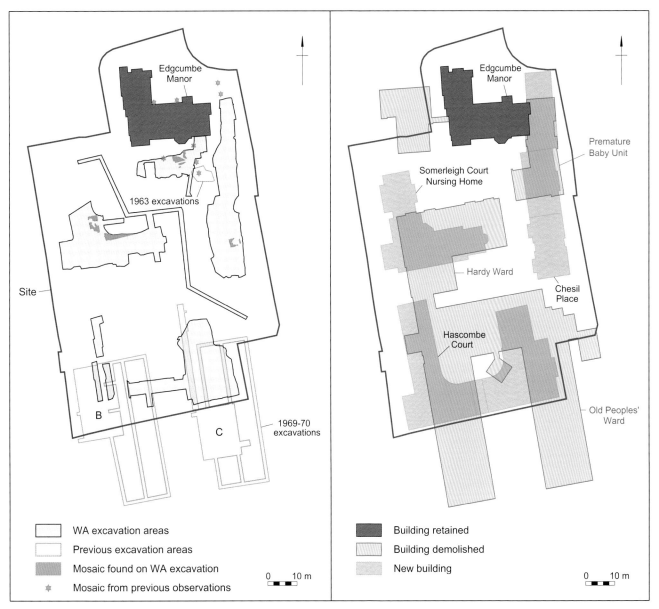

Figure 6: Location of the 2000-2001 excavation areas in relation to previous work and modern site layout showing the buildings post-redevelopment

Medical provision and care in Dorchester

Dorchester has a long tradition of provision of care. Records suggest the existence by 1324 of the Hospital of St John the Baptist (St John's House) - probably providing shelter for travellers and pilgrims but maybe some help for the sick as well. There may also have been a 'lazar-house' or hospital for the relief of lepers, though little detail is known. A workhouse or hospital, 'The Hospital of the Bailiffs and Burgesses of the Borough of Dorchester' was founded for children in 1617 but, eventually, different provision was required. By 1744 another workhouse was founded and in time that too was replaced (in 1837) by the Poor Law Union Workhouse, renamed in 1948 as Damers Hospital. Dorset County Hospital was founded in 1838 and designed by Benjamin Ferrey (Fig. 4). The hospital was designed on a symmetrical E-plan, although it looked like a gabled Elizabethan mansion (Newman and Pevsner 1972, 183), being built of Portland stone with pitched tile roofs, ashlar chimneys, and mullion windows (Fig. 5). Records from the Hospital (1838-1948) are held by the Dorset County Record Office, Reference Code: NG/HH/DO(C).

Historically, most of the people who were not nursed in their own homes stayed in someone else's and it took a very long time for hospitals to become commonplace. Many of the new hospitals of the 18th century - which often started life in converted houses rather than being purpose built, were charities like their predecessors - providing meals, beds and shelter for their mainly poor patients. During the 18th century it was pointed out in print (Foster 1768) that domestic buildings were not ideal but it was not until the end of the 1850s that the difficulties of hospital design became the focus of specialist attention in Britain (Stevenson 2000, 1-3). In addition to practical considerations (such as how to prevent contagion due to the gathering sick or infectious people together), moral and social issues were debated (such as the need for ornament in functional or charitable buildings).

Hospitals: *Dorchester, A History of the County of Dorset: Volume 2, 1908, 101-3*
http://www.british-history.ac.uk/ report.asp?co=40159

Draper 1992, 53-7
http://www.institutions.org.uk/ workhouses/england/dor/dorchester_ workhouse.htm

Figure 7: Somerleigh Court (now Edgcumbe Manor) during re-development

The scheme also entailed refurbishment of the increasingly derelict Somerleigh Court, which was converted for residential and administrative use. To mark its renovation, this was renamed Edgcumbe Manor, restoring a link with its original 19th century owners and honouring one of the hospital's former wards. However, in this report the use of the historical name Somerleigh Court has been retained to identify the Victorian house.

Roman Dorchester

The Dorchester area contains a wide variety of prehistoric monuments and artefacts but little pre-Roman evidence was found on the site so our story begins in the Late Iron Age (*c* 100 BC–AD 43).

By this time, Dorset, eastern Devon, western Hampshire, and southern Somerset formed the core territory of a people known as the *Durotriges*. These

Somerleigh Court

Somerleigh Court is a spacious and finely built grey limestone town mansion which originally overlooked its own extensive terraced and landscaped gardens to the south (Fig. 7). The house was erected as a private residence in 1862 by Dorset banker Edward Pearce. In 1829, Pearce's uncle, William Eliot, had made him a partner in the 'Weymouth Old Bank' (Messrs Eliot, Pearce and Co.), which rose to become one of Dorset's foremost financial institutions.

Pearce and Eliot both died in 1885, and the bank was taken over by Eliot's two sons, joined later by Pearce's son, Robert Pearce-Edgcumbe, who inherited Somerleigh Court from his father. Pearce Edgcumbe had trained as a barrister, was a social reformer, an unsuccessful Liberal parliamentary candidate and served as mayor of Dorchester in 1891. He was knighted in 1895, becoming Sir Robert Edgcumbe. In 1896 he agreed to pay the Eliots £10,000 to buy his way out of the bank but, shortly after (in March 1897), Eliot, Pearce & Co collapsed with liabilities of some half a million pounds. Bailiffs took possession of Somerleigh Court and its contents, and Sir Robert thereafter severed his ties with Dorset. He died in Cornwall in 1927 (Attwooll undated).

The house was absorbed into the Dorset County Hospital serving as the core of its maternity wing. An eastern extension was built in the early 1960s to house the premature baby unit and a western wing was added in 1965. Somerleigh Court fell into dereliction after the relocation of the maternity care provision to the new hospital and demolition of its east wing left the gable wall and roof cavity of the Victorian structure perilously exposed. By 2000, the unoccupied property was increasingly threatened by the elements and by vandalism. It was refurbished during the regeneration project and renamed Edgcumbe Manor.

seem to have comprised a loose feder-ation of associated groups rather than a politically coherent tribe, although a considerable degree of cultural unity is evident: the absence of a clear, domi-nant pre-Roman capital may indicate that the *Durotriges* lacked the cen-tralised leadership attested amongst Iron Age tribes to the east (Cunliffe 1974, 96–9). Many rural settlements are known, including locally at Fordington Bottom (to the west of the town), Maiden Castle Road (to the south-west) and Whitcombe (to the south-east; Penn 1980, 57), but the largest centres of occupation and prob-ably also of political power were hill-forts. Among these, Maiden Castle (Fig. 8) has often been assumed to have been paramount, because of its size (it is one of the largest in Europe, enclosing *c* 18 ha) and because it lay so conspicuously near the site later chosen for the Roman tribal capital, but other sites such as Hengistbury Head (which was an important trading port and Iron Age mint) and large hill-forts including Hod Hill, Ham Hill, Cadbury Castle and Badbury Rings may have been equally important, if not more so (Rivet 1970a, 48–50; Cunliffe 1974, 96–9). A large, low-

lying *oppidum*-like enclosure (fortified settlement) recently discovered south of Ilchester, remains incompletely understood (Leach 2001, 14–15).

History has bequeathed no written accounts of the *Durotriges*. They seem to have remained, to a greater or lesser extent, culturally distinct, if not isolat-ed from their eastern neighbours, the *Atrebates* of north Wiltshire, east Hampshire, Surrey, and Sussex, and maintained many of their own cus-toms. For instance, even though cre-mation emerged as the dominant 'romanised' burial rite after the Conquest, the *Durotrigians* continued to practise inhumation – burying their dead in a crouched position (Philpott 1991, 53). The *Durotriges* possessed distinctive ceramic styles and an important pottery production centre based around Poole Harbour grew to national importance at this time. Working of Kimmeridge shale into items such as jewellery, furniture fit-tings, and vessels, and the production of salt, are also attested as significant industries. Until the mid-1st century BC gold coinage was used, but this was abandoned in favour of silver and bronze, possibly to facilitate cross-channel trade with the tribes of the

Figure 9: Gaulish green glazed jar and detail of mosaic showing the high quality finish

Armorican peninsula (Cunliffe 1974, 96–9). *Durotrigian* coinage was unin-scribed and, unlike some other regions of Britain, the late pre-Conquest rulers of Dorset remain anonymous.

In AD 45, two years after the emperor Claudius's initial invasion of the British Isles, the Second Augustan Legion (*Legio II Augusta*) was able to begin its campaign to subdue the south-west (Peddie 1997, 136). The *Durotriges* were almost certainly one of the two 'powerful tribes' reduced to submission at this time (the other being the *Dumnonii* of Devon and Cornwall), and Maiden Castle was among the 'twenty towns' similarly reduced (Suetonius, Vespasian (4); Ireland 1988, 58). The suppression of British resistance in the south-west was completed within a decade, and the Second Augustan Legion decamped from its early base at Lake Farm, near Wimborne (Field 1992, 32–44) to a new fortress at Exeter in *c* AD 55 (Bidwell 1979, 1).

Figure 8: Maiden Castle Iron Age hillfort

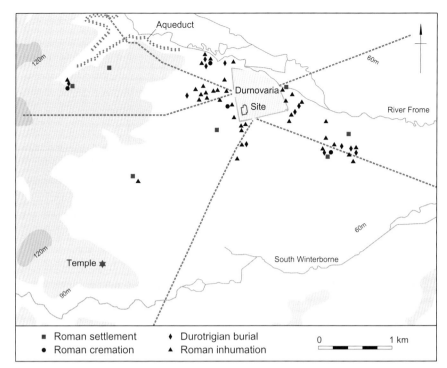

Figure 10: Roman Durnovaria showing the major roads, settlements and extra-mural cemeteries

By *c* AD 60–65, some 15–20 years after Dorset was first subdued, a new town of *Durnovaria* (Figs 2, 10) was laid out at the rounded eastern end of an approximately east–west aligned chalk promontory on the south-western edge of the Frome Valley. From a maximum elevation of just over 75 m OD at Top'O'Town, near the probable site of its west gate, the majority of the land on which the town was built sloped gently towards the Frome, or east and south-east into a dry tributary vale where a possible site for the Roman east gate has been suggested. At the south-eastern corner of the town the land rose again onto a rather smaller adjacent promontory, Fordington Hill.

Despite the long history of archaeological investigation, the origins of *Durnovaria* remain uncertain. Indeed even the name of the Roman town itself is not entirely certain: the widely accepted spelling is found in only one of several manuscript copies of the *Antonine Itinerary*, a late 2nd century 'road atlas' listing 225 routes across

the Roman Empire including a number in Britain. It is commonly assumed that the town was the administrative capital and market centre for the post-Conquest territory (or *civitas*) of the *Durotriges*, although Ilchester (*Lindinis* or *Lendiniae*) in south Somerset may have administered a northern subdivision of the *civitas* in

the later Roman period (Burnham and Wacher 1990, 69). Formal establishment of *Durnovaria* (in the sense that it gained recognised legal status) was probably preceded by a phase of less formal occupation and activity, which could account for some of the 'early' finds from the town. These objects include items said to have military associations, *Durotrigian*, Claudian, Tiberian and Neronian coins, 1st century Corfe Mullen pottery, pre-Flavian (ie, pre-AD 73/4) samian pottery and other imported wares including *Terra Nigra*, as well as a large assemblage of 1st century AD native-style brooches (RCHM(E) 1970, 533; Woodward 1993, 359). It has commonly been suggested that a military base or camp may have formed the nucleus of the early town (eg, Frere 1974, 74; Wacher 1978, 316; Field 1992, 125–34; Putnam 1998, 94), although no trace of this has been revealed from excavations. An early settlement might also have coalesced around the junction between the east–west road linking Exeter with southern and eastern Britain and a spur-road heading south over the Dorset Ridgeway to Weymouth harbour (Hinton 1998, 11). It has also been suggested that the position of the town (or of 'pre-town' occupation) could have been influenced by a pre-existing shrine or cult centre (Woodward 1993, 367).

In the mid–later 2nd and earlier 3rd centuries the town saw its most widespread growth and prosperity. During this period it was gradually refashioned, with substantial stone-founded houses dominating the street frontages in place of the early, often widely-spaced, timber buildings.

An unenclosed settlement for the first century or more of its existence, *Durnovaria* was furnished with earthen bank-and-ditched defences on its southern, eastern, and western edges in the later 2nd century. Along its northern edge, the nature of any defences remains unattested by excavation but any defensive work probably made use of the steep edge of the Frome Valley. The new defences were on a scale unparalleled amongst the towns of Roman Britain. A wide inner earthwork rampart (possibly with a timber palisade) was surrounded by three ditches measuring 15–20 m wide and over 4 m deep. Outside the ditches there is evidence for an external 'counterscarp' bank (observed, for example, at Southgate House and Dorford Baptist Church (Bellamy 2004)). These defences were augmented in the late 3rd or 4th century by the addition of a masonry curtain wall, built on top of the inner rampart (RCHM(E) 1970, 542–9). Immediately inside the defences, a zone of large quarries (see for example Patrick Greene 1993; Smith 1993) probably supplied additional chalk for construction of the rampart.

In the later 3rd and 4th centuries towns across Britain and the western Empire underwent profound changes. These were reflected in their layout and settlement structure, their function and economic importance, and in the evidence for their population density. At St Albans whole areas of the early town went out of use in the 4th century and, at Wroxeter, the forum was neither cleared nor re-occupied after the 3rd century. Similar evidence for urban decline comes from towns including Exeter, Cirencester, Chichester, Winchester, and even London (Wacher 1978; Reece 1980, 78–9).

Grand, lavishly appointed, urban houses were still built by wealthy citizens at this time, but these were often sparsely distributed and sometimes associated with their own complexes of agricultural and/or industrial buildings that suggest farming of cleared 'brownfield' land, rather than classic town life. Whilst some administrative function probably remained vested in towns, they seem increasingly to have became little more than defended centres for their territories (Millett 1992, 221). Even in London, blankets of 'dark earth' formed in parts of the

Town layout

Around *Durnovaria*, approach roads are known from the east and west, from the south and south-east, and from the north-west, although in no instance has their exact point of entry into the town been found archaeologically (Figs 2, 10). It has long been suspected that the east–west aligned main street (the *decumanus maximus*) must have lain somewhat south of modern High West and High East Street, although recent work at Dorford Baptist Church (just outside the supposed position of the west town gate) revealed evidence for defensive features (Bellamy 2004) and may require the axis of the main street to be sought yet further south, nearer the surviving fragment of Roman wall in Albert Road. Equally, the *forum* (the town's market place and commercial centre) and *basilica* (its administrative offices and public meeting hall) have never been identified with certainty but are believed to have lain near the town centre in the Cornhill area, where gravel-metalled surfaces have been noted (RCHM(E) 1970, 564–6). A recent interpretation of the town's layout (Woodward *et al.* 1993, 360, fig. 173) suggests the *decumanus maximus* dog-legged around the western and southern perimeter of the *forum* and *basilica*, with its eastern section corresponding more closely to the alignment of modern Durngate Street than to High East Street.

The town's public baths lay beneath Wollaston Field (now the Wollaston long stay car park and adjacent Social Services building; English Heritage in prep.) *c* 300 m east of the site and may have been associated with a temple or cult centre, as was famously the case at Bath (*Aquae Sulis*) (Woodward 1993, 361). The amphitheatre at Maumbury Rings, just east of Weymouth Avenue, has curiously early origins, possibly as a *ludus* or military training area. It seems to have become disused before the end of the 2nd century; in the 3rd century three adults were buried in the silted up ditches (Bradley 1975). It has no known replacement within or around the town.

town during the 3rd and 4th centuries, and the population of the city seems to have declined significantly from the levels attested in the 1st and 2nd centuries (Marsden 1985, 101, 104).

Few names are known from *Durnovaria*: a 2nd century tombstone was reused beneath the porch of St Georges' Church at Fordington is most probably from the Roman cemetery there. It records the death of Carinus, a 50 year old Roman citizen. His memorial was set up by his children Rufinus, Carina, and Avita, and his wife Romana (RCHM(E) 1970, 574). Elsewhere, graffiti scratched into wall plaster from the 4th century Colliton Park townhouse reads *Paternus scripsit* (Paternus wrote [this]) (Putnam undated, 12). From Greyhound Yard several names are known from graffiti on pottery – ALBUS, IULIA or IULLA, TACITUS, PRIMUS, NUTRIX (literally wet-nurse but probably used here as a personal name) (Tomlin 1993, 284–5).

Rather greater information on the town's Roman inhabitants and their state of health has been gained from their skeletal remains, excavated from the many individual graves and cemeteries which surround the town. From the present excavations there are a number of infants who had been buried within the town (see below). Evidence for early surgery has been found locally at the cemetery at the Poundbury trading estate, on the edge of the Frome Valley just to the south-east of Poundbury hillfort (Sparey Green 1987; Farwell and Molleson 1993, pl. 52).

Cemeteries excavated at the Crown Buildings site, between Bridport Road and Poundbury Road, (Esmonde Cleary 1987, 70; Wessex Archaeology 2007b) and Poundbury both indicate the presence of a significant Christian community within the town in the 4th century. Those buried here may have included followers of the British-born Pelagius, whose teachings gained popularity amongst the ruling elite of early 5th century Britain. Pelagianism, which maintained that through the exercise of human will, each person can become the architect of their own salvation without dependence on the grace of God (essentially refuting the notion of original sin), was declared heretical by Pope Celestine. Such was the concern of the Church that it sent a delegation including Germanus (later St German), Bishop of Auxerre, and Lupus, Bishop of Troyes to *Verulamium* (St Albans) in AD 429–30 to counter the heresy (Frere 1974, 367–9).

Within Dorchester itself, evidence for a change in urban character in the later Roman period came from the excavations, and a similar sequence of change is documented in other nearby excavations, including Greyhound Yard and Colliton Park (Woodward 1993, 369), and possibly at Charles Street. At the Wollaston Field baths, a large and important building was maintained into the 4th century (Esmonde Cleary 1989, 72), although this survival might have been linked with a temple complex (Woodward 1993, 367), rather than perpetuating an existing public amenity.

As with many Roman towns, there is only slight evidence for the latest occupation and eventual abandonment of *Durnovaria*. Rare structural evidence for this period was discovered on the northern part of the hospital site, where a wooden building was constructed over street 178 (see below; Wacher 1978), which must by that time have been disused (Hulka and Hodgson 2000; Cox forthcoming). Further to the east, at Greyhound Yard, a soil interpreted as an arable ploughsoil was noted, sealed below post-Roman dark earth (Staines 1993, 314).

There is evidence that the southern part of the town (at least) was being farmed as early as the 7th century (Woodward 1993) but the impact of this on the hospital site, if any, is unclear. Despite the development of medieval and post-medieval Dorchester, probably after the 10th century (Penn 1980, 60), land in the south-west corner of the former Roman town remained agricultural or horticultural in character until the 19th century when the County Hospital was constructed. In the later 20th century, the site was again altered by construction of new hospital buildings.

Previous archaeological work

The Roman street which lies immediately east of the site is listed by the Royal Commission on Historic Monuments (England) (RCHM(E) as monument 178 and is hereafter referred to by this number. Its ENE–WSW alignment was established during construction of an annexe to the south wing of the main County Hospital building in 1949, where it was just over 6 m wide with a cambered profile up to 0.3 m thick. Two courses of flint nodules packed in loam and separated by a thin layer of redeposited chalk formed its base, and its main surface was 'metalled' with flint and gravel. A late resurfacing took place after *c* AD 330 (RCHM(E) 1970, 552). More recently street 178 was seen during excavations north of Somerleigh Court (Hulka and Hodgson 2000; Cox forthcoming).

Construction of an eastern extension to Somerleigh Court in 1963 exposed parts of two masonry-walled rooms, separated by what may have been a vaulted passage or cellar. The more fully exposed northern room was probably originally semi-sunken, with a limestone flag floor, but had been partially infilled and refloored with a coarse 'tessellated' pavement of red tile and grey limestone, bearing a design of linear bands and chequerboard squares. Its internal wall plaster had been painted with a series of panels. A doorway was set into the south wall, and here the design of the floor suggests the room may have formed a north–south passage, with a lost partition wall, or even a staircase to the east, where there was no evidence for tessellation (Cosh and Neal 2006, 109). The construction date of the building was not closely defined, but 1st and 2nd century pottery was found filling the vaulted passage, indicating a

A remarkable tale of survival

Despite the ravages of medieval and post-medieval stone-robbers, 19th century landscape gardeners, and those who constructed, then demolished the 20th century hospital buildings, the site's Roman archaeology was uncommonly intact and legible by comparison with many Roman towns in Britain. The building plans that were obtained were, with one exception (Building 7), remarkably complete (Fig. 11).

Set near the edge of the Roman walled town, the site remained outside the core areas of medieval and early post-medieval settlement, which lay along High East and High West Streets, South Street and (presumably) around the medieval castle (now occupied by Dorchester prison). Trinity Street and Princes Street both developed as back lanes or passages behind the medieval burgage plots along the South Street and High West Street respectively. The south-west quarter of the town remained largely undeveloped, used only for agriculture and horticulture. Eighteenth and earlier 19th century mapping of the town shows the show this was the case until Somerleigh Court was built in the 1860s. The site has also been cushioned from later damage by the deep late Roman, post-Roman, and later dark soils that developed across the southern part of the old town.

More problematic for the site's analysis was the nature and composition of the Roman archaeology itself. Many of the soil layers encountered had not formed *in situ*, but were dumped in the Roman period, to create building terraces or make-up construction levels beneath buildings, to raise or level the contemporary ground-surface, or as bedding for hardstandings and yard surfaces. An analysis of conjoining samian sherds from the extensive Greyhound Yard excavations confirmed the considerable extent to which Roman soils and finds were redeposited away from their point of deposition (Woodward *et al.* 1993, 369–70).

At the former County Hospital site similar layers often contained large and interesting groups of finds, amongst which were highly unusual objects such as fragments of 'tazza' (thought to have been libation cups, lamps, or lamp-holders for burning incense), a near-complete imported fineware pottery lamp (Fig. 34), a gold finger-ring (Fig. 38) and many fragments of vessel and window glass, but the value of these items for dating the deposits that contained them, or as a guide to the activities which were actually being carried out on the site in antiquity, was limited. These soils and the materials they contained

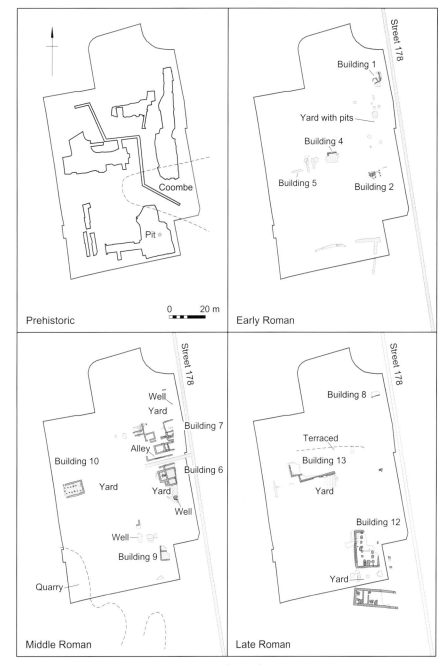

Figure 11: Main excavations showing the major phases of activity

could have been redeposited from sites anywhere within (or even outside) the Roman town. Deposits which had definitely formed on the site and, therefore, contained finds which help to understand how the site was used, were scarce by comparison. Key amongst these were early Roman pits from Chesil Place and 4th century features from Hascombe Court which are discussed below.

middle Roman date. The lack of diagnostically 4th century finds suggest the building had become disused by the late 3rd century although, on stylistic grounds, a 4th century date for the inserted floor remains possible (Cosh and Neal 2006, 109). Later observations immediately south of this building record parts of another structure and, to

11

Figure 12: TV camera filming the mosaics

the west, a small walled yard with a thin cement floor overlying mid-2nd century pottery sherds (C. Sparey Green, pers. comm.; RCHM(E) 1970).

A western extension to Somerleigh Court built in 1965 revealed evidence for quarrying inside the town defences, and possibly for the existence of a building (Stephenson 1998, 27).

In 1969 two trenches were excavated prior to the construction of three large new hospital buildings (the Old Peoples' Ward; Fig. 6). The western excavation (Trench B) only produced evidence for ditches, and for quarrying inside the town rampart but Site C (to the east) was rather more informative, revealing part of a range of 3rd–4th century agricultural or industrial buildings. Numerous small stone-built ovens had been inserted into this at a late stage in its use, although no evidence was found to indicate exactly what these were used for. In striking similarity to the Hascombe Court excavations (2000–1, reported on

below), typically late Roman pottery and a dispersed hoard of late Roman (AD 370–402) coins were scattered throughout the reworked post-demolition soils within the confines of the building, suggesting that its use may have extended into the early decades of the 5th century (Patrick Green 1993; Cooke 2007). A long trial-trench (Trench 3) dug northwards from Site C, alongside what were, at the time, tennis courts, partly coincided with the 2000–1 excavation. A small trial-excavation east of the site (beneath what is now Weld Court) produced evidence for successive and short-lived 4th century buildings, and for a medieval structure (Wilson 1971, 279).

In the early 1980s, construction of the Hardy Ward passed without any provision for archaeological observation or record being made. It was the foundation trenches dug at this time which destroyed parts of the geometric mosaic in Building 13, beneath the Nursing Home.

During the 1980s and 1990s, various small pieces of work were carried out, the closest of which was on the line of Somerleigh Road, immediately north of Somerleigh Court, where modifications to the road gradient required a reduction of existing ground-levels. Two adjacent Roman buildings were found, their use spanning perhaps two centuries (Hulka and Hodgson 2000, Cox in prep.).

Little information about the Roman buildings along the eastern frontage of street 178 exists as archaeological levels beneath what is now Somerfield supermarket were largely removed, but the remains of a stone-founded domestic building and tessellated floors were recorded during construction of the Forum Centre shopping arcade in Trinity Street (Wessex Archaeology 1994).

The 2000–2001 excavations

The former County Hospital site comprised almost 0.80 ha within the Roman town's south-western quarter, and situated between the rear boundaries of Somerfield supermarket and car park, and properties along West Walks (Fig. 3, centred on NGR 369070 090455). Its northern extent was marked by a dog-leg in the alignment of Somerleigh Road adjacent to the western end of Alexandra Terrace, and additional public car-parking lay immediately south of Hascombe Court.

Within the redevelopment area, just over 1700 m^2 were subjected to detailed archaeological investigation (Fig. 6). Following national planning guidance, excavations were conducted only where new building and infrastructure would damage or destroy archaeological deposits. Whilst this has left many questions about the site unanswered, it has ensured that irreplaceable parts of the town's archaeological heritage have been preserved for the future.

The areas excavated corresponded as closely as possible with the construction footprints of the proposed new buildings but factors, such as the presence of live buried services, and a requirement to leave unexcavated strips next to standing buildings and beneath the canopy of a mature Holm oak tree, constrained the available working space in some places.

In the public eye: public involvement, public access and the media

Public involvement in the process of archaeology has been increasingly recognised as a desirable element of fieldwork and these excavations provided an excellent opportunity to draw local people into the excavation process. Through the auspices of the

Portable Antiquities Scheme it was possible to tap into a body of expertise and enthusiasm amongst several local metal-detecting societies, with entirely positive results. The artefact and coin lists from the excavation attest a notably more thorough recovery of coins and other metal objects than might otherwise have been the case.

Discovery of the mosaic floors beneath the Somerleigh Court Nursing Home sparked local and regional media interest, in the press (with headlines such as '*Mosaics mayhem hits town*', Dorset Echo, 23 July 2001) and on television (Fig. 12). In July 2001, Bentleigh Cross Ltd. funded a site open day to provide the public with an opportunity to view the excavation on the Somerleigh Court Nursing Home site and the mosaics which had been exposed there. Exceeding predicted visitor numbers by a considerable mar-

gin, an estimated 5000–6000 people passed through the site during the day (Fig. 13), most having waited for several hours in a queue that stretched out to Trinity Street. Despite this comments in the visitors' book and the wealth of praise on the day confirmed the depth of continuing local interest in Dorchester's Roman origins.

Pre-Roman activity

The earliest Roman levels commonly lay above a layer of reddish–brown clay–loam. Similar layers have been recorded on other excavations in and around Dorchester (eg Draper and Chaplin 1982, 27; Adam *et al.* 1992; Staines 1993, 313–14; Bellamy 2004) and represent vestiges of the pre-Roman ploughsoil.

A single prehistoric feature was discovered south of Somerleigh Court. Pit

or tree-throw hole G.740 (Fig.11) probably pre-dates the latest stage of prehistoric ploughing, evidence for the latter has been identified on other local sites. Burnt material including fragments of sandstone had been dumped into it. Sandstones do not occur naturally immediately around Dorchester, but quernstones of this material have been found in the locality (eg Wessex Archaeology 2007a).

Prehistoric flintwork was recovered from the site including a probable Lower Palaeolithic flake (500,000–150,000 BC) and a later Mesolithic (*c* 6500 BC) microlith or projectile point. These would not originally have been discarded in the deposits in which they were found and as such cannot provide direct evidence for activity on the site at these periods.

Figure 13: Queuing during the open day

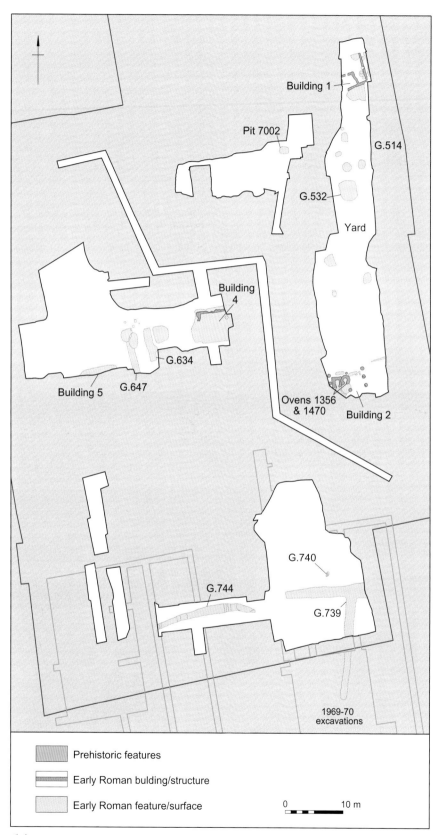

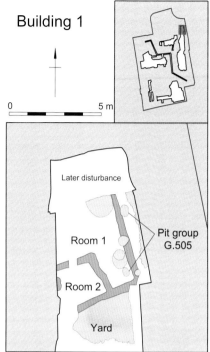

Building 1

0   5 m

Figure 15: Detail plan of Building 1 and overlying pits

Development of the Roman town 1st to mid–2nd century AD

In common with other sites in Dorchester (eg Woodward *et al*. 1993), early Roman buildings on the site were of timber construction, founded either on ring-beams or earth-fast posts. Semi-cellared buildings of a type seen on rural settlements around the town (Barnes 1997; Davies *et al*. 2002) were also found. Artefacts of mid-1st century date included pre-Flavian items, key amongst which were pottery including *Terra Nigra*, Corfe Mullen wares and Gaulish green-glazed wares and four coins (Fig. 17) copying official issues of the emperor Claudius (AD 42–54). These imported pots were very different to those that had been used up to this point, bringing new colours and a quality which had not been seen before.

Figure 14: Early Roman phase plan

Prehistoric features

Early Roman bulding/structure

Early Roman feature/surface

0   10 m

Early Roman activity along the street-frontage

At the northern end of Chesil Place, an arrangement of infilled beam-slots had been cut into the reddish–brown pre-Roman or early Roman soil horizon. These formed the south-eastern part of a timber-founded building (Building 1, Figs 15–16) measuring in excess of 4 m by 5 m. The alignment of Building 1 reflected the NNW–SSE axis of street 178, which lay immediately to the east, just beyond the edge of the excavation. No evidence for the function of Building 1 was found, but domestic use would seem most likely. Its construction date could not be established except in broad terms. It could date from as early as AD 60–65 (pre-Flavian timber structures were identified at Greyhound Yard (Woodward *et al.* 1993)).

Demolition, clearance and levelling of Building 1 probably took place in the early–mid-2nd century, after which a number of small pits were dug in the area (G.505; Fig. 15). These in turn were then buried beneath successive spreads of grey loamy silt and redeposited chalk, probably forming a garden or yard associated with middle Roman Building 7. At an even later date, the northern part Building 1 was destroyed by construction of semi-sunken Building 8.

Figure 17: Copied coin of Claudius, dia. 26 mm

Figure 16: Building 1

A 1st century timber dwelling

The remains of Building 1 (Figs 15–16) comprised two steep-sided and flat-based slots at 90° to each other, up to 0.45 m wide and 0.25 m deep. These would have held horizontal wooden beams supporting a timber-framed superstructure, probably of single-storey design and perhaps infilled with wattle and daub panels. No roof tiles were noted here and the building may, instead, have been thatched, or roofed with pegged wooden shingles.

The southern foundation slot probably supported the external wall. Immediately to the south there was a yard surface consisting of a layer of small nodular flints firmly set in rammed chalk. The proximity of the street edge at this end of the site (perhaps no more than 1–2 m away) suggests that the eastern foundation slot marks the front of the building. Another ragged area of nodular flint cobbling lay 0.3–0.6 m east of this, and could be an area of external hardstanding on the street frontage itself.

Inside Building 1, a shallower and more irregular arrangement of slots indicateed internal partitions, possibly forming small rooms and/or a corridor. No internal plaster was present and neither were there any internal floor-surfaces. Depending on the function and status of the building, its floor may merely have been of compacted earth (perhaps with straw or rushes), or possibly raised timber boards.

Early counterfeiting?

Figure 17 illustrates a poor quality contemporary copy of a copper coin (*as*) of the emperor Claudius (AD 41–54), one of four such coins to come from Chesil Place. Copies of this type have been found on several sites in and around Dorchester (eg Bradley 1975, 74–5; Reece, 1993, 116; Aitken and Aitken 1982, 105) and they illustrate the scarcity of these low denomination bronze coins in northern Europe and Britain between AD 42 and 64, after which the emperor Nero circulated large quantities of newly minted bronze coins (Boon 1988, 119–23). The theory that copies of Claudian bronze coins were produced by the Roman army as 'quasi-official' small change has gained popularity in recent times and their occurrence is still sometimes taken as evidence for a military presence (eg Wacher 1978, 316). A counterargument which takes into account the often very poor quality and reduced size of many copies, suggests the coins were produced by the civilian population for their own use. Whatever their origin, the coins seem to have been tolerated (or perhaps expediently ignored) by the provincial authorities, and allowed to circulate freely because their use enabled the state to recover and recycle the gold and silver currency which it paid out to its military and civil service.

Claudian copies quickly fell out of use after Nero's recoinage in the mid-AD 60s, although the value of the Chesil Place examples for dating the site is lessened by their recovery from spreads of dumped soil that could have been imported from elsewhere in the town at a later date. However, their presence does add to the growing body of evidence for pre-Flavian (pre-AD 73/4) – and possibly pre-town – occupation.

Figure 18: Reconstruction of amphora used to transport oil, wine and fish sauce to Britain; Dressel 2-4 amphora (left) and Dressel 20 (right)

Yard

South of Building 1, an extensive yard or open area appears to have remained undeveloped in the early Roman period. It may have been used for small-scale horticulture or penning of livestock. A dispersed scatter of pits (Fig. 19) was clearly used for the disposal of domestic rubbish and pit 7002 contained silty grey, cess-based fills, indicating is use as a cess-pit.

The largest of the pits in this yard area (G.532) was sub-rectangular in plan and may have been a well or waterhole. It measured 3 x 3.5 m, and was evidently of considerable depth. Only its uppermost fills could be excavated safely. Around its edges, indistinct slots dug into the natural chalk bedrock may have marked the position of a timber well-head. After its disuse, the waterhole was infilled; a 2nd century coin was recovered from these deposits. Continued slumping of the deposits used to backfill G.532 caused long-term structural subsidence in part of the overlying middle Roman Building 7.

Figure 19: Plan of pit group south of Building 1

Early Roman rubbish pits

Pit group G.514 (Fig. 19) provided some of the most securely stratified dating evidence for the early Roman phase, and the pit fills are amongst the few deposits which can confidently be shown to result from on-site activities. The pits were not all open at the same time and may not have been functionally related but they form a closed stratigraphic group, buried beneath a middle Roman yard surface. Detailed study of their finds suggests sequential use, perhaps over a number of decades.

The earliest pit (1547) was probably infilled during, or shortly after the third quarter of the 1st century AD. Jars and bowls made by the South-western Black Burnished ware industry accounted for over half the pottery, while vessels from the local Wareham/Poole Harbour kilns represented only 14%. A piece of pale green vessel glass and sherds of fine, brightly-coloured pottery vessels imported from the Continent were very new elements in the range of domestic goods available to the inhabitants of *Durnovaria*, the likes of which they had never seen before. As well as the shiny, translucent glass, these included bright red, glossy cups and bowls in south Gaulish samian ware, a silky-smooth, black *Terra Nigra* dish and a leaf-green (lead-glazed) beaker from Central Gaul. Fragments of a Spanish Dressel 20 amphora (Fig. 18), used to transport olive oil, as well as oyster shells and animal bones from sheep/goats, cattle, and pigs indicate something of the foods being eaten at this time.

Approximately 90% of the pottery from Pit 1439 also consisted of everyday food preparation, serving and storage vessels in Black Burnished ware fabrics, 60% from the South-western kilns and 30% from the Wareham/Poole Harbour region. Thin-walled, white flagons made at Corfe Mullen were also unusual at the time, not only for their colour (white pottery had never been made in Britain before) but also because they were the first wheel-thrown vessels to be made in the area. Imports included samian from South Gaul, a 'rusticated' fineware cup from Lyons, north-western Gaulish mortaria (mortars for grinding), and more Dressel 20 amphorae. The animal bones were dominated by cattle and sheep/goat but also included pig, domestic fowl, and fish scales and bones. Charred grains of wheat of varieties known as emmer and spelt may have been associated with malting and brewing in the vicinity. Other, more personal, items included a broken brooch, part of a shale bracelet, and a copper alloy coin, a *dupondius* of Trajan, dated to AD 98–117. Collectively, these finds suggest a closing date at around the end of the 1st century AD.

Sherds of South-east Dorset Black Burnished ware outnumbered those of south-western origin in Pit 1481 although the range of vessel forms was again typically early, with upright necked and bead-rim jars, round-bodied open bowls in the Maiden Castle 'war cemetery' style, and imitations of Gallo-Belgic forms. Part of another north-west Gaulish mortarium was found, along with sherds of Dressel 2–4 (wine) amphorae (Fig. 18), and a second green-glazed beaker from Central Gaul.

The latest pit (1434) may have remained in use until the second half of the 2nd century. Here, South-western Black Burnished ware was in the minority and the pottery assemblage included small amounts of residual Corfe Mullen ware, other oxidised wares, a Dressel 20 amphora fragment, and a piece from samian bowl decorated in the style of the potter Attianus who worked at Lezoux in Gaul around AD 125–145. Oyster shells and bones from sheep/goats and pigs represent butchery waste but the only other finds from this feature consisted of building rubble – stone and fragmentary ceramic bricks and roof tiles.

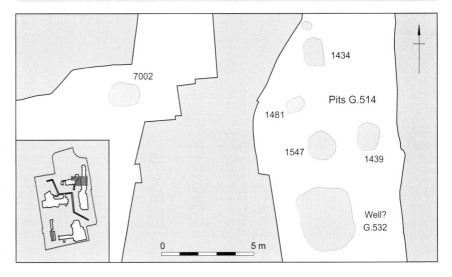

Early agricultural/industrial activity north of the coombe

A cluster of early Roman features was identified beneath the Somerleigh Court Nursing Home. Pits, ditches, postholes, shallow gullies and parts of two semi-cellared buildings (Buildings 4 and 5) all probably indicate agricultural or low-level industrial activity. Amongst these, ditch (G.647) may have been a boundary, possibly to separate buildings 4 and 5. Immediately to the east of this, a shallow, flat-based ditch G.634 (Fig. 14) contained a deposit of deliberately set flint nodules, possibly a structural footing for the gable-end of an otherwise unrecognised timber building.

Sunken, or semi-cellared Building 4 (Figs 20–21) was identified at a late stage in the excavations, and its presence explained a history of local subsidence and remedial dumping which had been charted in later Roman hard-standings or yard surfaces directly

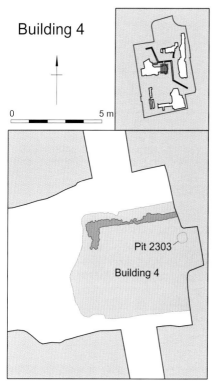

Figure 21: Detail plan of Building 4

above. Its superstructure was probably originally of timber and it may have been provided with a suspended wooden floor, as no steps were seen and there was no evidence for wear or 'trample' on its base. Fourteen metres to the west, the northern end of what may have been a second sunken building (Building 5) was seen. Measuring just over 5 m wide and at least 0.5 m deep, this may have been either a smaller sunken building, or one of similar dimensions, but set at right-angles to Building 4.

At the end of its use, Building 4 was deliberately dismantled. The remaining hollow was infilled with numerous dumps of soil and discarded building materials; a fragmentary stone mortar was found amongst this material. Later (possibly as a prelude to the laying of a rubble-metalled yard) the remains of Building 4 were more comprehensively buried under a widespread dump of grey–brown silty clay containing 1st and 2nd century pottery.

Figure 20: View of the excavations showing early Roman Building 4 in foreground

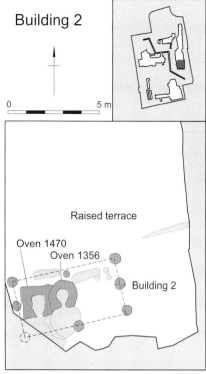

Figure 22: Early ovens and post-built Building 2

Building 2

0   5 m

Raised terrace

Oven 1470

Oven 1356

Building 2

Figure 23: Two early ovens 1470 (left) and 1356 (right)

At the southern end of Chesil Place the northern shoulder of the coombe was deliberately levelled-up with dumps of chalky brown clay. Sometime after the terrace was created two stone-lined ovens were dug into its surface (Figs 22–23). These were conjoined but had clearly not been built at the same time. The deeper, eastern, oven (1356) was later than its shallower western counterpart (1470). Thin and patchy lenses of redeposited chalk and charcoal-rich soil adjacent to the ovens may have been the remains of contemporary working surfaces.

The function of the ovens remains unknown but there is no evidence that they were industrial and they may have been used for cooking or baking. The soils which filled them after they went out of use contained charcoal that seemed to have come from green or damp wood. This might have been deliberately chosen to lower firing temperatures or, perhaps, to increase

the amount of smoke produced. These layers also included large numbers of very small fish bones. These are of small herrings and probably also of sprats. Bones from both the head and body are frequent and it is estimated that 600–700 individual fish are represented by these remains (Fig. 24). These fish would have been very small (less than 110 mm long). This suggests that the fish bones are the remains of

allec, a sauce made by fermenting very small whole fish (Curtis 1991), usually made in the Mediterranean region but there is increasing evidence for local production in other parts of the Empire (van Neer and Lentacker 1994) including London (Bateman and Locker 1982), York (O'Conner 1988), and Lincoln (Dobney *et al*. 1996). This deposit from Dorchester is the most western example in the northern

Fish sauce

Although not necessarily to modern British tastes, the popularity of *garum* and other fish sauces in the Roman world is well attested: of nearly 500 recipes listed by the Roman culinary writer Apicius, over 400 include its use (*Encyclopaedia Romana*). Interestingly fish sauces were used in medicine to treat both humans and animals. Pliny and Celsus list a range of disorders that different fish sauces were used to treat (Pliny, XXX1.96ff; Celsus, II. 29).In the Mediterranean world, a variety of fish sauces were produced by allowing vats of brine or salt, and fish, sometimes whole and sometimes just the entrails, to ferment in sunlight. In temperate Britain artificial heat would have been required for the process. It is likely that countless regional and local variants with differing additional ingredients and preparation methods would have been used across the Empire. The production of fish sauce would have been undertaken on an industrial scale given its popularity.

A recipe for *garum* is given below. This differs from *allec* in that it uses larger filleted fish, whilst *allec* was made from small whole fish. However the basic method is the same:

Garum
Ingredients: Sardines, herrings or pilchards, strongly scented herbs (such as dill, coriander, fennel, celery, mint, or oregano), salt

Method: Place a layer of herbs into a large jug. Remove bones from fish and mash the flesh. Place a layer of fish on top of the herbs. Add a layer of salt to the depth of two fingers. Repeat the layers of herbs, fish, salt until the jug is full. Leave for seven days then turn daily for the next twenty days by which time it will have liquidised and it is ready for use.

http://www.romans-in-britain.org.uk/arl_roman_recipes-garum_fish_sauce.htm
http://www.penelope.uchicago.edu/~grout/encyclopaedia_romana/wine/garum.html

Figure 24: Fish bones - the remains of allec or fish sauce

Figure 25: A fragment of imitation samian ware, possibly central Gaul. Note the unusual decorative motif representing a theatrical mask suspended on a pole

Early Roman ovens

Stone-lined hearths, generally referred to as ovens, have been found on many Roman sites in and around Dorchester (eg Aitken and Aitken 1982; Patrick Greene 1993; Wessex Archaeology 2007a). Similar in form to the updraught kilns used for making pottery, these typically comprised a pit within which a fire would have been set. Heat from the fire was drawn through the oven structure via a flue into a circular or U-shaped firing chamber – where, presumably, a sealable opening allowed items to be inserted for heating – then upwards through a vent. Rarely does any evidence for the superstructure survive and different forms of oven may have served many widely differing functions.

Oven 1470 was set in rectilinear construction pit and was built of undressed limestone slabs, bonded with pale yellow chalky-clay paste. Its relatively shallow firing chamber (0.30 m deep) was concave in profile and fully lined with limestone. Its interior surface had been discoloured to a dark blue-grey indicating exposure to relatively high temperatures. Its fire-pit was immediately to the south and had been modified during the oven's period of use, having been made narrower by dumping soil outside a new lining of vertically-set limestone slabs. Oven 1356 was of a more typical 'hourglass' plan. Also built from limestone slabs and chalky-clay paste, its conical sub-circular firing chamber was 0.55 m deep and steep-sided. The base of the chamber was of bare, natural clay. Its edges were altered in places to a dull orange-red by exposure to rather lower temperatures than the other oven. This difference in discolouration may have resulted from variations in the flow of heat through the different designs of oven and may not reflect the working temperatures they achieved.

Roman Empire and, as such, is of some importance. Although it is unlikely to represent fish sauce production within the town – as it would have been a smelly process – the deposit may represent the discarded residue or remains of a spoilt product that had been made on the coast.

After the ovens had been levelled, a rectangular building (Building 2) was erected over their remains. Measuring at least 6 m by 3 m, seven large circular post-pits and a collection of associated features including shallow 'slots' attest a timber post-built structure. The function of the building remains unknown, but the absence of other building materials from its setting suggests that its fabric was of wood, or wattle and daub panel, and that its roof that was thatched or shingled, rather than tiled.

Activity south of the coombe

In the early Roman period, the site lay on, or near the periphery of the town's developed area. On the south slope of the coombe, T-shaped ditch G.739 and similarly aligned ditch G.744 may have formed part of a system of small fields or stock pens near the edge of the settled area (Fig. 14). The lower fill of ditch G.739 produced a fragment of human pelvis, belonging to a male, aged around 45–60 years at death. Burial of individuals other than infants was forbidden within the bounds of Roman towns and it is possible that the bone is of pre-Roman date.

The south end of ditch G.739 was excavated in 1969, when it was attributed to the mid-1st century AD (Patrick Greene 1993, 73). Several other ditches beneath the western part

Figure 26: New Forest Parchment ware candle-stick with red painted slip decoration

of Hascombe Court contained inade-quate dating evidence and could not be phased, but these collectively indicate that this part of the site remained unde-veloped throughout the Roman period. At least two of these features were later than ditch G.744.

Food and dining

Evidence for food and its consumption came from the site throughout the period of occupation in this part of *Durnovaria*. The remains of fish sauce or *allec* was found (see above) and other marine resources were also exploited, including oysters, cockles, carpet shells, limpets, whelks, razor shells, and scallops. The oysters were not specially selected and may have come from natural uncultivated beds, possibly in Poole Harbour. Overall, the shellfish only augmented the diet, rather than formed a significant part of it. A probable mollusc pick was recovered from the site (Fig. 27). Animal bones were found in some quantity, the main domesticated species being represented (cattle, sheep/goat, pig, and domestic fowl). There was limited evidence for the exploitation of wild species but some game (hare and deer) and wild birds (mallard, wigeon, woodcock, and songbird), may have been consumed. Animal bone evidence indicates that pigs were bred and slaughtered in the town, a pattern noted at other sites in Dorchester (eg Maltby 1993). The neonate remains of cattle and sheep indicate that some were kept locally while others were brought into the town for slaughter. Secondary products (wool and milk) and the use of animals for traction would also have been important to the inhabitants. Eggshells and the remains of goslings and chicks show that they were probably kept in the town for their eggs, meat, and feathers. There is evidence that the town's inhabitants also farmed the surrounding land (Woodward *et al.*1993, 375).

Charred plant remains also provide an intriguing insight into the supply of food to the town. Quantities of charred grain together with lentils and weed seeds, including bitter-vetch, were found in several contexts. Although the evidence is relatively slight, it is likely that some of this material was imported from the Continent, a picture that finds parallels in London (Straker 1984), although greater quantities of locally produced food would undoubtedly have been used. Other food items show that grapes, sloes, hazelnuts, and apples were consumed. The recovery of amphorae shows that wine, fish sauce, and oil were imported from Spain, France, and other areas of the Empire, although there is also evidence for vineyards being established in Britain and for the local production of fish sauces (see above).

Artefacts from the site also provide some insights into the dining habits of the townspeople. Items such as the imported fine ceramic tablewares, mortaria, lamps (Fig. 34), glass vessels, three copper alloy spoons, and the mollusc pick were clearly available to the residents of *Durnovaria* soon after the Conquest, but it is difficult to be sure whether they reflect the adoption of Roman customs and culinary tastes or were merely fashionable curiosities to the largely native population of the town. Gradually, the local Purbeck industries began to copy such Romanised items, producing shale tables, trays, and platters and imitating the shapes of imported pottery vessels.

Some of the late Roman artefacts also reflect the level of sophistication seen in the buildings with their painted wall plaster and mosaic floors. By this time, lighting was provided by candles, probably of tallow or beeswax, set in very modern-looking candlesticks (Fig. 26). A piece of glass decorated with an etched fish (Fig. 28), probably part of a scene depicting Neptune, dates from the first third of the 4th century and comes from a shallow bowl which may have been made and engraved, using diamonds, around Cologne, Germany. Pliny (*Natural History* book XXXVII, xv, 61) mentions Germany as the source of the best diamonds and this vessel would have been a very expensive and exotic item.

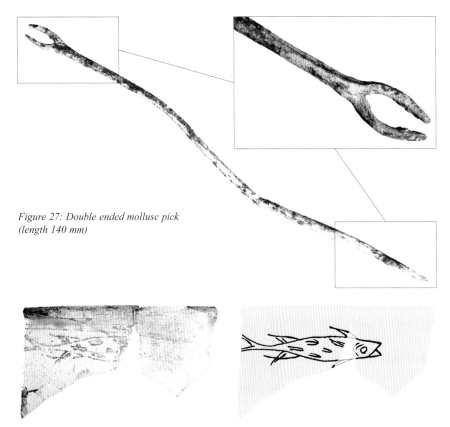

Figure 27: Double ended mollusc pick (length 140 mm)

Figure 28: Fragment of glass vessel decorated with a fish etched design

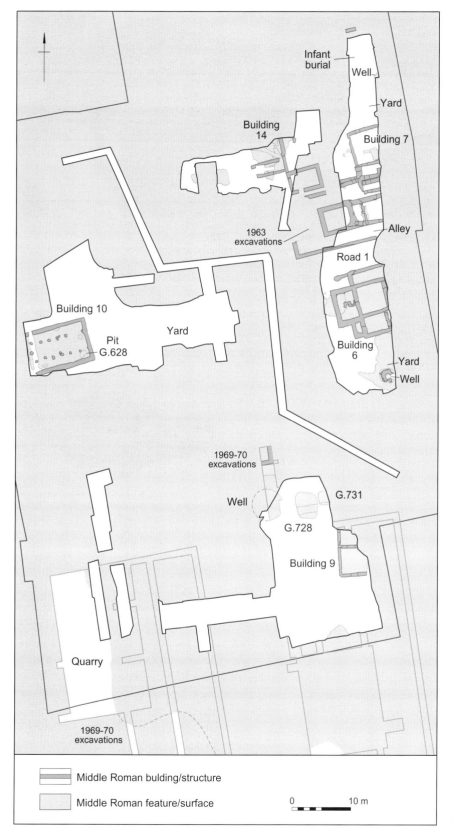

Figure 30: A rare very finely carved Roman bone mural crown hairpin from Chesil Place (figure height 26 mm)

At some time after AD 130, but more probably in the later 2nd century, *Durnovaria* was enclosed by a broad belt of defensive earthworks (RCHM(E) 1970, 535). It is tempting to see their creation as a major impetus for the redevelopment of the site, as land which formerly lay on the exposed edge of the town became a safer, higher status, and more attractive prospect. Probably in the mid–late 2nd century, relatively comfortable and well-appointed town houses were constructed along the western frontage of street 178. Parts of three such houses were excavated. Land to the west, in the interior of the *insula* (block of buildings within a Roman town), was occupied by at least one industrial or agricultural building (Building 10) and crudely-surfaced open areas or yards.

Figure 29: Middle Roman phase plan

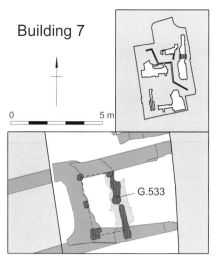

Building 7

0 _____ 5 m

G.533

Figure 31: Plan of Building 7 showing early
phase posts G.533

Robbed out walls

Figure 33: Southern part of Building 7

Middle Roman buildings along the western frontage of Street 178

Northern property (Building 7)

The central part of the Chesil Place excavation area had suffered particularly badly from dissection by modern foundations and drain-runs, as well as from more general medieval or post-medieval stone-robbing (Fig. 32–33). This, along with a number of poorly understood modifications to Building 7, made its ground plan impossible to establish with any certainty. Despite these problems, it was clear that one wing of what may have been a town house of some grandeur, size, and importance occupied this part of the

Figure 32: Later Roman well/fountain head
and deposits associated with yard

site. The remnants of deep, mortared foundations below a robbing trench perhaps attest a substantial superstructure, although the walls of this range further to the east were based on much more ephemeral footing courses. The remains of Building 7 can be linked directly with those recorded by Dewar and Aitken in 1963 and by Sparey Green soon after and so, indirectly, with Building 14 immediately south of Somerleigh Court (see below). This house may have surrounded a garden or open area (seen as a sequence of interleaved and layers of redeposited grey loam and chalk) known as an *atrium*. This was a very typical roman house plan in many parts of the Empire. Within this area was part of a mortar well-head or possibly a decorative feature such as a fountain (G.502, C. Sparey Green pers. comm.). This appears to have been an early feature of the putative garden; a chamfered mortar fillet surrounded its base, and subsequent dumps of soils appear to have built-up around the structure. An infant burial was also discovered toward the base of the external soil sequence and pottery and coins throughout were generally of 1st–2nd century date.

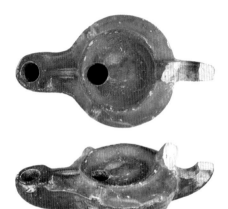

Figure 34: Gaulish ceramic lamp (length 92 mm)

The earliest precursor of Building 7 may have been of timber-post construction (Fig. 31). An indistinct but generally rectilinear arrangement of probable post-settings (G.533) was seen beneath the stone-built walls and footings. Although these could belong to the earlier Roman period, the close accordance of their layout with that of the main wall footings suggests that they should be accepted as part of the middle Roman developmental sequence.

South of Building 7, a *c* 2.5 m wide band of redeposited soils may have lined a path or alley. These were closely defined to the south by the mortared

Figure 35: Building 7 showing chalk-founded annexe

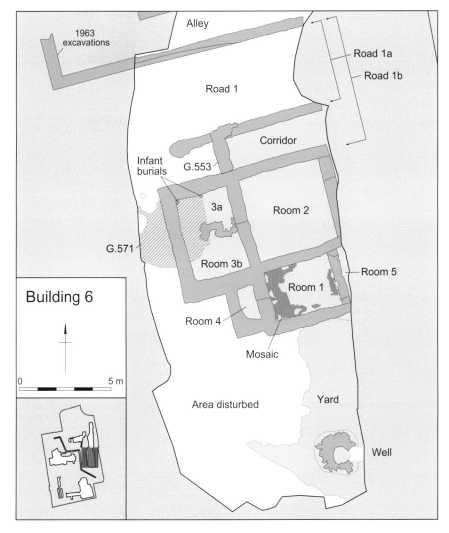

Figure 36: Detailed plan of Building 6 including yard and road 1

flint footings of boundary wall G.549 (see description of Building 6 below). The near-complete imported pottery lamp (Fig. 34) was recovered amongst these soils.

Late in the history of Building 7, a new room or annexe was added. Extending into the open area to the north, its narrow rectilinear foundation was butted onto a pre-existing mortared stone wall to the south (although this had subsequently been robbed-away and its presence was inferred only from a medieval or post-medieval soil-filled trench). This foundation trench, packed with chalk rubble and chalk-paste (Fig. 35), probably supported a wooden-framed building.

Figure 37: Samian 'gladiator' sherd (figure height 35 mm)

Central property (Building 6) and Road 1

Early Roman Building 2 was probably demolished and cleared by the 2nd century, after which additional dumps of soil were widely spread over its remains. The abundant finds from these deposits included much South-eastern Dorset Black Burnished ware, and lesser amounts of South-western fabric, samian (Fig. 37), Lyons and central Gaulish wares, as well as south Gaulish or Spanish pottery. British regional imports included mica-dusted wares, 'London-type' ware, and Exeter legionary fortress ware. Two joining sherds from separate contexts from a

23

Figure 38: Gold finger ring, internal dia. max 21 mm, equivalent to modern ring size S–U

tazza represent an unusual find from the town, one of three such vessels from the site. All of the finds except for three intrusive late pottery sherds were of late 1st to mid-2nd century date. Also recovered were many fragments of plain and coloured vessel and window glass, a gold finger-ring (Fig. 38), which was originally fitted with a gem or carved *intaglio*, and the only domestic cat bone from the site. A curious subcircular patch of *opus signinum* (fine Roman concrete) (G.571) lay adjacent to the western edge of the trench, where it was cut by the foundations of Building 6 (Fig. 40). Measuring approximately 3.5 m across and 40 mm thick, it had a gently sloping surface. No evidence for walls or retaining structures was found around its edges, and it is unlikely to have been the floor of a building. It may represent nothing more significant than an external hardstanding or working area, or even a dump of unwanted waste concrete.

Building 6 was domestic in character (Fig. 36), although rather smaller

than the sprawling Building 7 to the north. An arrangement of three rooms (Rooms 1–3) and a small annexe (Room 4) represent the rear part of the building. Of these, Room 1 retained parts of a decorative tessellated and mosaic floor, which had been extensively damaged and patched in antiquity. There was no hypocaust and the mortar sub-floor lay directly on earlier soils. Little remained of the room's central mosaic panel, but the fragments which did survive are unparalleled among British mosaics. It has been suggested that this may have been laid by local builders, rather than by a specialist mosaic-maker (S. Cosh, pers. comm.).

The damaged mosaic in Room 1 was directly sealed beneath a deposit of broken Purbeck stone roof tiles with some flint and limestone pieces. Although it is tempting to see this as evidence for the decay and collapse of the building, the fact that not a single complete tile was recovered may, instead, point to a rather more systematic dismantling of its superstructure, with recovery of re-usable materials and discard of broken tiles. Below this

layer were hints of a more generalised rubble-levelling deposit. What may have been an inserted shallow (single course) flint footing (1362) bisected Room 3 and may indicate a phase of subdivision (Rooms 3a and 3b).

Figure 39: Detail of mosaic panel corner

Figure 40: Patch of opus signinum hard-standing

Building 6

Building 6 was founded on footings of nodular flint solidly packed in stiff clay, set in foundation trenches up to 0.50 m deep and as much as 1 m across. The rear part of the building was seen, comprising three rooms and a northern corridor. A small room or ancillary structure (measuring about 1.5 m by 2 m) nestled in the angle formed by the western and southern rooms.

The house had employed stepped-level construction to accommodate the very gentle gradient of the site, and any former floor layers within Rooms 2 and 3 had been destroyed by later activity. Parts of a decorative floor survived in Room 1 (which measured 3.4 m by 2.7 m) (Fig. 39, 41). Set onto a base of yellow mortar, this comprised a coarse red tile tessellated surround, probably deliberately speckled with paler yellow and blue-grey. This was about twice as wide to the north as it was to the east and west and, if a correspondingly wide border existed along the southern edge of the room then the central mosaic panel was probably square. Most of this panel had been destroyed in the Roman period, but two small corners survived, showing this to have been of relatively crude workmanship. It was edged with a thin line of very dark blue/grey and, inside this, both corners had a small square of red, both with a 'quincunx' (like the number 5 on a dice) arrangement of five white tesserae. The red squares were surrounded by white, speckled with individual dark tesserae, but no other evidence of the design survived (Cosh and Neal 2006, 114, no. 165.42). The bedding mortar beneath the eroded parts of the floor was worn and pitted and some small areas of deeper damage had been patched with compacted layers of marly chalk and very dark soil, one of which contained a coin of Probus (AD 276–282). Two low portions of standing wall at the northern and southern edges of the room were of mortared flint and limestone above a single, externally offset, course. No evidence for doorways was seen although, if the room was accessed from the north, there may have been a single step down from the adjacent Room 2.

Particularly good dating evidence came from the dump of broken stone roof tiles that filled Room 1. Among seven coins were three copies of 'Gallic Empire' radiates (dated to AD 270–290). More significantly, two radiates of Carausius (AD 286–293, Fig. 56, and two *quinarii* of his successor Allectus (AD 293–296, Fig. 56) perhaps indicate demolition in the last few years of the 3rd century or the earliest 4th century.

Figure 42: Early phase yard surfaces with well

Two infant burials were found close together against the interior of the northern wall footing of Room 3 (Fig. 36). It is unlikely that the graves, which comprised little more than small scoops excavated against the interior wall-line, were put in place whilst Building 6 was in its heyday and it may be that they date to the second half of the 3rd century, or to the earlier 4th century, by which time the status of the house had declined considerably. Burial of infants within buildings in Roman towns was a common practice (see below).

Butting against the southern wall of Building 6 was an expanse of open metalled yard or hardstanding (Fig. 42). This had been resurfaced on a number of occasions throughout the later 2nd and 3rd centuries, first with fine, clean gravel which had been patched with crushed mortar. Above this, a layer of crushed stone tiles lay

Figure 41: Tesselated floor in Building 6

Figure 43: Original well head masonry

beneath a surface of flat-laid broken stone roof tiles. Finally, a layer of dark loam had been laid down, onto which had been set a hardstanding of flint nodules, bedded three courses deep and firmly packed in more dark loam. Ten radiate coins (including copies, dated AD 270–290) came from the dark bedding soil, with a coin of Valerian/Gallienus (AD 260–268) and a residual *sestertius* of Hadrian (AD 117–138) from amongst the courses of flint. Some 4th century pottery from this layer might indicate that the flint yard surface of late Roman date, but this contrasts with the complete absence of 4th century coins. The reason why such a massively thick hardstanding or yard was built here remains a mystery and certainly points to very heavy-duty usage. It could relate to the latest phase of use of Building 6, perhaps no longer of domestic function. A well was maintained throughout the yard's period of use, and its original unmortared stone well-head or fountain (Fig. 43) had been rebuilt to remain above the rising ground-level. The zone immediately to the west was deeply truncated by later disturbance and the original westerly extent of the surface remains unknown.

Immediately north of Building 6, a minor road (Road 1) was probably a private track providing access between street 178 and land on the interior of

Figure 44: Building 6 – demolition of north corridor

Figure 45: Road 1b showing wheel-ruts

Figure 46: Painted plaster fragments

the *insula*. In its early stages its surface comprised a thin mortar layer and spreads of compacted chalk. At this time the track was just over 4 m wide (Road 1a), and was bounded to the south by the corridor on the northern edge of Building 6. Later, this corridor was shortened, and its formerly open western end was blocked with a new closing wall (G.553). After this, the corridor was dispensed with altogether and its north wall demolished (Fig. 44). Further compacted chalk surfaces (Road 1b) overlay its footing making the track just over 6 m wide. Irregularly parallel sets of wheel-ruts were noted, at this level, attesting to the passage of wagons or carts (Fig. 45). The final remetallings of the track were worn and survived only along its central spine. These comprised up to 50 mm of fragmented wall plaster (including with some painted decoration, Fig. 46), fragmented mortar, and a number of rough, unused limestone *tesserae* blanks or rejects.

Southern property - Building 9

Building 9 lay near the eastern edge of the Hascombe Court excavations, and represents the rear portion of a stone-founded property (Fig. 47–48). The presence of *in situ* green painted wall

plaster here points to a domestic function. No floor surfaces survived, but a patch of finely-crushed ceramic tile fragments in the south-west corner of the northern room (Room 1) may be the only surviving trace of a sub-floor. The almost north–south to east–west axial alignment differed from the dominant trends north of the coombe, but perpetuated that of the 1st century ditch G.739 (see above) which may have remained as a vestigial earthwork.

Immediately behind (west) of Building 9, pits G.731 and G.728 seem to have been broadly contemporary with its period of use. Pit G.728 was subrectangular (measuring 4 m by 3.5 m) and could not be fully excavated. It may have been the shaft of a well.

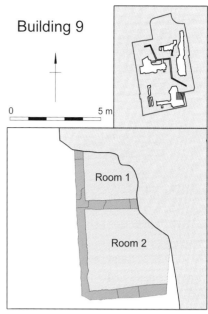

Figure 47: Detailed plan of Building 9

Figure 48: Building 9

A similar large pit (pit 2) was reported by Patrick Greene from immediately west of the excavation, where the corner of an adjacent 2nd–3rd century stone-walled building was also exposed. Both of these features were believed to have fallen into disuse by the end of the 3rd century (Patrick Greene 1993, 86–7).

Building 14

In September 2001 it emerged that plans to build a paved terrace immediately south of Somerleigh Court would require construction of a new retaining wall. The initial design involved cutting a deep foundation trench along the existing terrace but had not taken into account the high quality, well-stratified Roman remains known to survive in this part of the site. In particular, part of a 3rd or 4th century geometric polychrome mosaic was exposed in about this position in about 1862–3 (Moule 1906, 33–4), and exhibited for a visit to Dorchester by the British Archaeological Association in 1864 before being reburied (Cosh and Neal 2006, 110, no. 165.34).

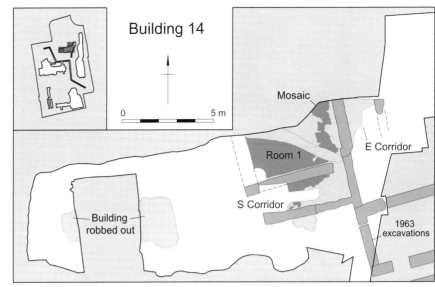

Figure 49: Plan of Building 14, southern part of building extrapolated from 1963 excavations

Figure 50: Building 14 tesselated floor detail showing 'cut-out' centre

Building 14: recording for preservation

At the western end of the trench only dark rubbly soil was seen, although there was a subrectangular area of mortared limestone-slab floor (Fig. 49). An indistinct zone of less rubbly soil around this feature might indicate the positions of medieval or later wall-robbing trenches.

Better-preserved building remains lay to the east. Well-mortared masonry walls defined a rectangular room measuring 5 m by at least 3 m, set within the angle formed by two passages or corridors, each 1.4 m wide. As with Dewar and Aitken's (1963) building to the south-east, this room had evidently been modified several times. Its latest floor surface comprised a remarkably crude, unmortared tessellated pavement of grey limestone with some seemingly randomly-distributed red ceramic tesserae, all ranging in size up to 40 mm by 30 mm. Below this were patches of dark loam and a thin mortar floor, which may have been an earlier surface rather than a bedding course. Dark soil was noted again underneath the mortar surface. At the southern edge of the room the tesserae partially overlay lengths of *opus signinum* 'quarter-round' coving. This itself butted against degraded wall-plaster (Fig. 51) and was probably not an original feature of the room. Fragmentary coving was all that remained to mark the position of the robbed out western wall.

An unusual feature of the late floor was a roughly quarter-circular 'cut-out' in the south-west corner of the room (Fig. 50). This was clearly intentional rather than resulting from later damage as its edge was formed from a single arc of tesserae. The most likely explanation is that the floor was laid around an existing architectural fitting that has since either decayed or been removed. The southern passage was distinguished by a comparatively well-executed and well-worn tessellated floor of dull red tile, although much of this had been destroyed by a modern concrete drain. To the south, a small patch of well-sorted flint nodules in a chalk matrix may have been either internal or external flooring. The eastern passage was floored only with a thin skim of mortar but, further to the east, a line of red tesserae above yellow bedding mortar and a rubble sub-base was seen in the edge of the salvage area, attesting yet another room or corridor.

No diagnostically late pottery came from Building 14 and, of the three coins recovered from dark soils immediately above the latest floor, one was of mid-3rd century date and two were issues of Carausius (AD 286–293). As with Building 6 to the south-east, this suggests the latest use of the buildings was in the very late 3rd century, or perhaps the earliest years of the 4th century. The 1862–64 mosaic was not found in the expected location and, if not destroyed during the 1980s, may remain intact further to the north.

Figure 51: Building 14, late floor overlying earlier elements

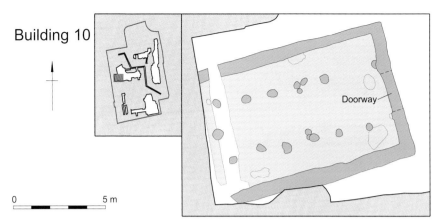

Building 10

0   5 m

Doorway

Figure 52: Detailed plan of Building 10

Roman Building 14 was recorded and the retaining wall was redesigned to rest on a minimally destructive piled footing, allowing preservation of the remaining archaeology *in situ*. Archaeological remains were protected under terram membrane and clean sand before the new terrace was laid over them.

The interior of the insula: 'cob-built' barn (Building 10)

At the far western edge of the Somerleigh Court Nursing Home, a lower status building may have served an agricultural function, or accommodated domestic slaves or servants. Building 10 (Figs 52–53) was 7.5 m wide, internally *c* 6 m, and was at least 10.75 m long, although its western end lay beyond the excavated area. Wall-footing trenches up to 0.75 m wide and up to 0.22 m deep (shallower on the northern, uphill side of the structure)

Figure 53: Aerial view of Building 10, note the stone threshold in the centre

Figure 55: Internal stone floor-slab, Building 12

Figure 54: Copper alloy double-twist finger ring, dia. 22 mm (top), Copper alloy plate brooch, length 34 mm (middle), Head stud, this may originally have been tinned or silvered, dia. 23 mm (bottom)

had been solidly packed with pale yellow–brown chalky clay, possibly cob. In two places, soft-spots in the underlying natural chalk had been carefully dug-out and firmly repacked with flint nodules before this was laid. A well-built limestone slab threshold (Fig. 53) 2 m across was set centrally in the eastern gable end, and two parallel rows of post-holes lay along the axis of the structure. A thin, worn and patchy clay floor surface lay below a thicker internal deposit of collapsed cob, which contained some unpainted plaster and 3rd–4th century pottery.

Located inside the walls of Building 10, but probably of earlier date, was a shallow sub-rectangular pit (G.628) that yielded mid-Roman pottery. Its lower fill also contained quantities of hammer-scale, a by-product of iron smithing, indicating that this activity was occurring close by.

East of Building 10, a series of soil, chalk, and rubble spreads with 2nd–3rd century pottery made up an extensive yard (Fig. 29). Adjacent to Building 10 (where there was a natural rise in old ground levels) these layers had been destroyed by later construc-

tion work but, toward the eastern end of the trench, their upper surface was compacted and worn, attesting a long period of exposure and use. Pottery evidence from the surface suggests it remained in use until the later 3rd century.

Coins of Carausius (AD 286–293) and Allectus (AD 293–296) (Fig. 56) were found in disuse deposits immediately above two of the middle Roman buildings (Buildings 6 and 14), suggesting that, at this time or shortly thereafter, the site underwent a major change of use and probably ownership.

Figure 56: Coins: Carausius, dia. 22 mm (left) galley on reverse of Allectus quinarius, dia. 20 mm (right)

Changing times: the late Roman period (late 3rd to early 5th centuries)

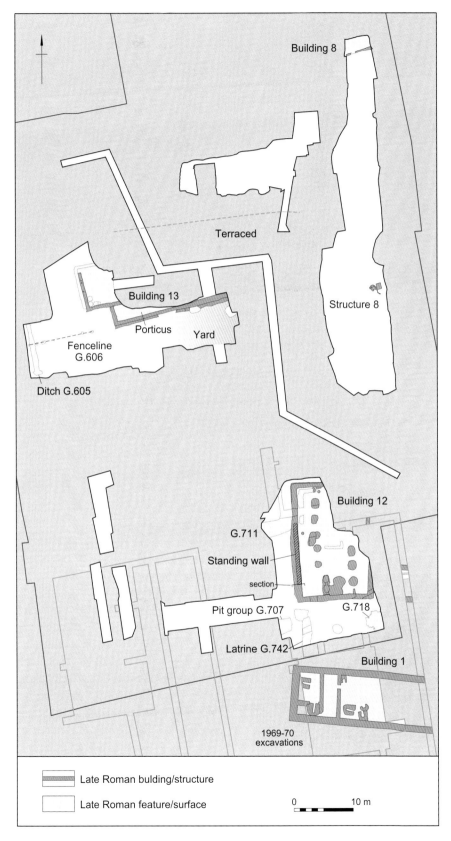

Late Roman bulding/structure

Late Roman feature/surface

0   10 m

By the 4th century the structure of many Roman towns had changed, for reasons which are not fully understood (Reece 1980; Esmonde Cleary 1989, 64–85) (Fig. 57). From many towns (including Dorchester) there is evidence for widespread clearance of domestic housing (see above) and the construction in its place of a lesser number of new buildings. Some of these were domestic houses, often betraying the great wealth of their owners, but others were lower-status structures, built to serve agricultural or industrial functions.

It has been suggested that, in Britain like the rest of the Empire, the transformation of towns into what have been described as shrunken administrative villages can be charted throughout the 3rd century, corresponding with the waxing economic importance of rural villa estates. The 3rd century was a time of economic and military crisis in the Empire as a whole and in Britain the economy may have become moribund. Early imperial encouragement and support for development of towns in the far provinces through loans or tax concessions faded as costs, including defence of the Empire's borders, drained the imperial exchequer. Towns may have suffered as the well-off moved to new villas in the countryside. Concurrent with this there may have been a drift of less well-off rural populations into towns where there was the promise of money to be made but little real opportunity for success in a stale economy (Reece 1980, 87–8).

Figure 57: Late Roman phase plan

Structure 8: a 4th century 'working area'?

Built flush into the north-eastern corner of Room 2 within the now demolished Building 6 was a small 'working area' (Structure 8, Fig. 58). Here a low, roughly rectangular, platform, step, or structural base measuring c 1 m by c 0.8 m and constructed of limestone pieces bonded with loose, sandy clay-paste, incorporated a fragment of a carefully-dressed, fine sandstone window or door jamb (Fig. 59), a partially dressed rectangular limestone block, and part of a crude, broken niche or small trough. A Purbeck marble mortar (Fig. 59) was recovered from an overlying layer. Immediately to the west, an area of coarse paving had been fashioned from tabular limestone. Integral with southern edge of the rectangular platform was a c 1 m long crescent of thin, irregular limestone slabs set on edge, possibly surrounding a slight hollow. This may also have been originally floored with limestone but the evidence for this was much-damaged and inconclusive. Most of the area, particularly above the paving, was sealed beneath a thin layer of dark soil. Ten bronze coins of the House of Constantine were recovered from this dark soil and another three similar

Figure 58: Structure 8, possible working area

coins were found between the paving stones. If associated with its period of use, these date Structure 8 to c AD 343–348 or shortly after: coins of Valens and Valentinian, from the mid-AD 360s, were absent. Whether the coins represent a small scattered hoard, unrecovered coins from a larger single loss, or items lost individually over the working life of the structure, remains unknown, as does its overall function. Given the presence of architectural fragments and coins other possibilities might be considered, such as the presence of a small shrine.

Figure 59: Architectural fragment, length 220 mm (above) Purbeck stone mortar, length 180 mm (left)

Later Roman Building 8

A sunken, concrete-lined masonry structure was discovered at the furthest northern extremity of Chesil Place (Building 8, Fig. 60). Although stratigraphically 'late', its construction cannot be closely dated, and its purpose remains a matter for speculation. It lay at right-angles to the axis of the adjacent street 178, corresponding with the dominant structural alignments in the northern portion of the site, but neither the eastern nor western ends lay within the bounds of the trench. Given the proximity of street 178 at this point, the structure cannot have projected more than perhaps a metre or two further to the east. The floor and internal wall surfaces had been sealed with a single thick skim of hard *opus signinum* and the junctions of the floor and walls were marked by quarter-round coving. The interior surfaces of the walls also bore numerous triangular pecking marks, as if keyed for a secondary render or relining and the floor was much eroded and pitted. The floor adjacent to the eastern site edge had actually been punctured in this way, exposing the rubble sub-base below.

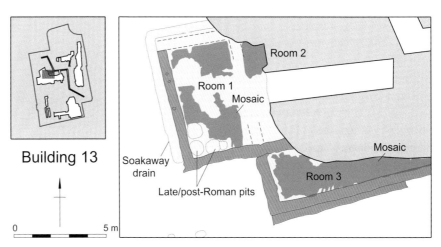

Building 13

Soakaway drain

Late/post-Roman pits

Room 1

Mosaic

Room 2

Room 3

Mosaic

0   5 m

Figure 61: Detailed plan of Building 13

Filling the remains of Building 8 was a dark rubbly soil that had presumably been dumped as a levelling deposit after its demolition. This contained nodular flint, limestone, stone and ceramic roof tile fragments, pottery, animal bone, oyster shell, and several hundred loose (and often worn) limestone and ceramic tile *tesserae* of varying size, indicating the contemporary destruction of a tessellated floor elsewhere. A coin of Theodora indicates that Building 8 cannot have been infilled before AD 337–341.

Building 13

The close association of a wealthy town house (Building 13) and a complex of agricultural or industrial buildings to the south (Building 12 and structures identified by Patrick Greene (1993)) is interpreted as part of a single intra-mural farmstead. Other such late Roman establishments have been suggested at Colliton Park and Greyhound Yard (Woodward 1993, 369). The construction of a large town house replacing the demolished domestic buildings of the middle Roman period (Building 13) implies that, by the 4th century, the site had come into the possession of a wealthy person. Building 13 (Fig. 61) perpetuated the dominant WSW–ENE structural trend seen in earlier phases of the site, but was set back some 25–30 m west of street 178, in an area formerly occupied only by open rubble-surfaced yards and at least one industrial or agricultural building (Building 10). Its construction first involved the excavation of a broad, flat platform into the chalk of the gently rising hill-slope, and this action destroyed any earlier archaeological remains over a considerable area of the site. At its western end, the new terrace had initially been strewn with small

Figure 60: Building 8 showing the concrete lining

pebbles which were pressed into the surface of the chalk; the reason for this is not entirely clear.

Regularly sized, vertically-sided and flat-based foundation trenches (0.5–0.6 m wide and *c* 0.4 m deep) were then cut into the bedrock, almost certainly to hold large wooden sill-beams. Above these, the superstructure of the house was probably timber-framed (perhaps with wattle and daub panel infill) set beneath a typically late Roman Purbeck limestone-tiled roof. The two easternmost rooms of the house (Rooms 1 and 2) bore the remains of elaborate and particularly finely-made polychrome mosaic floors (Figs 64–70). To the west, other chalk-cut beam-slots and remnants of mortared masonry cross-walls were observed in a trench dug to house a new sewer. Here the thin, tattered, and very extensively denuded remains of a mortar floor were also noted but there was no remaining evidence to indicate whether additional mosaics ever

Building 13

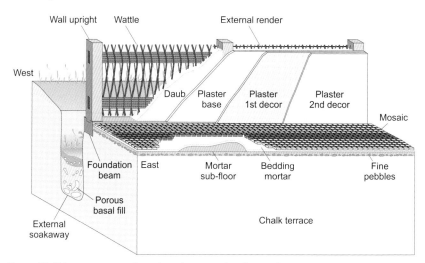

Figure 63: Schematic section through triclinium and soakaway drain

existed there. The use of masonry for the stubs of cross-walls to modify a timber-framed building initially seems curious, but would have presented fewer logistical difficulties than the insertion of a new timber footing.

A *porticus*, or possibly an open-sided arcade, along the southern edge of Building 13 (Fig. 64) was furnished with a tessellated floor of alternating red and grey longitudinal stripes, set on thick mortar bedding. This was over 16 m long but its eastern end seems to have lain beyond the area excavated.

Mosaics

In some parts of the building the original mosaic flooring and its underlying bedding mortar had been destroyed or eroded in antiquity and deposits of fallen painted wall-plaster had then accumulated. This plaster demonstrates that at least two decorative schemes had existed. The earlier was white, some fragments having a thin olive green line. The second layer was also white, but decorated with panels edged in a thin green line above a thin band of red, orange, and yellow, set

Figure 62: Excavating the mosaic

Building 13 mosaics by Stephen R. Cosh
Rooms 1 and 2

The western end of Building 13 seems to have been occupied by a divided room, floored with a fine mosaic pavement (reconstructed in Figure 64). This was executed in tesserae of dark blue-grey, blue-grey, pale blue-grey, and white stone, and red and yellow ceramic tile, all averaging 12 mm across. A border around the mosaic was in pale grey and red tesserae of about 30 mm.

The best-preserved part of the mosaic (Panel A, Fig. 68) lay in Room 1. Here there seems to have been insufficient space for a coarse border to exist along the eastern edge of the Panel, and this may indicate that the room functioned as a *triclinium* (a dining room, with space for three couches arranged around the bordered edges and facing the opening through the dividing wall). This arrangement was popular in the mid-4th century. Instead a narrow intermediate mosaic panel (Panel B, Fig. 70) lay to the east. This did not extend to the width of the adjacent panels, and may be assumed to indicate the position of responds (short protruding walls), which may originally have supported an arch. Panel C, to the east in Room 2, was only partially exposed but paved what is normally the larger, square part of such a divided room. However, a modern foundation trench had destroyed the eastern edge of Panel A, along with the flooring and/or walls between it and Panels B and C, making reconstruction of the room less than certain.

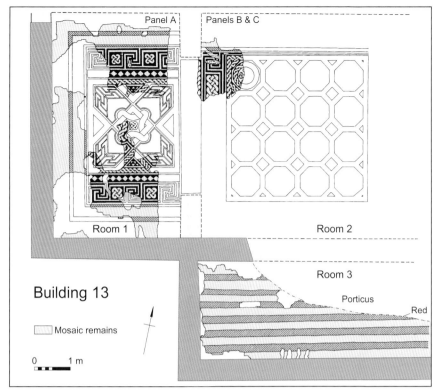

Figure 64: Reconstruction drawing of mosaics within Building 13

Figure 65: Painted plaster showing keying (Room 1 Building 13) collapsed over mosaic floor

The Porticus mosaic

This mosaic paved a south-facing *porticus* (corridor/veranda) 2.50 m wide by over 16 m in length, and comprised six bands of red alternating with grey. The floor was executed throughout in coarse tesserae (30 mm) and the bands varied in width: those in grey (7–9 rows of tesserae) were generally wider than the red ones (5–7 rows). Other corridors and passages in Dorchester with red and grey bands are known from townhouses at Colliton Park and Glyde Path Road, both of which are datable to the mid-4th century.

Figure 66: Mosaic from Building 13 (Panels B and C)

over a lower zone of deep red and blue/purple (Fig. 65). The secondary scheme had been keyed in preparation for replastering, although it seems that no tertiary skim was ever applied.

Immediately outside the western and northern walls of Room 1, a vertically-sided and flat-based trench, up to 1.1 m deep and 0.6 m wide is likely to have been a soakaway or drain. It was filled with loose, porous mortary sand, nodular flint, broken ceramic roof tiles, and contained a red deer skull (Fig. 63). Its existence indicates the use of a timber beam foundation for Building 13: the stability and structural load-spreading offered by a jointed

Figure 67: Conserving the mosaic

Panel A
(Cosh and Neal 2006, 112, no. 165.39)

In Room 1 was a square panel, of which only parts near the margins and traces of the centre survived. The scheme was a saltire (St Andrew's cross) formed by triangles on each side of a square frame delineated in simple *guilloche* (rope-like bands) outlined dark blue-grey with strands of blue-grey, pale blue-grey, and white (except on all three sides of the triangles where they alternated with strands of red, yellow, and white). Pairs of lozenges occupied the arms of the saltire; all the surviving ones had traces of swastikas in dark blue-grey. The two surviving triangles at opposite ends had unusual chessboard patterns of dark blue-grey isosceles and right-angled triangles. Only one very damaged fragment of the centre of the mosaic remained. This had traces of a curved band of *guilloche*, seemingly interlaced with another which formed two sides of a small white triangle. The probable reconstruction is a poised square interlacing with a cushion-shape. A leaf is all that remained of the filling motif in the odd U-shaped interspace in the arm of the saltire. There were also two curved double fillets of dark blue-grey and traces of rows of white and yellow, perhaps from a central *guilloche* knot. The square panel was flanked on the north and south sides by bands of opposing stepped-triangles (creating rows of poised squares with serrated sides), and spaced swastika-meander developing two squares on each side occupied by *guilloche* knots. The whole panel (4.20 m by 2.60 m) was bordered by a double fillet of coarse red tesserae and, up to the room's wall foundation slots, grey tessellation interrupted by a narrow band of red. The mosaic displayed good workmanship and, where undisturbed, an exceptionally smooth finish.

Figure 68: Painting of mosaic from Building 13 (Panel A). Plans to display the mosaic are currently being discussed

Panel B (Cosh and Neal 2006, 113–14, no. 165.40)

Only the edge of this survived, but enough was visible to show that it was a band (or mat) of *guilloche* shaded alternately as in the simple *guilloche*, but the strands have extra rows of red and blue-grey; this was possibly an intermediate panel marking the boundary between Room 1 to the west and Room 2 to the east.

Panel C (Cosh and Neal 2006, 113–14, 165.40

The decorative scheme of Panel C was probably a grid of octagons within a square (or rectangular) frame, delineated in simple *guilloche* outlined dark blue-grey with strands alternating red, yellow, and white, and blue-grey, pale grey, and white. Part of one octagonal compartment was uncovered, containing a circle of simple *guilloche* (shaded as before) enclosing a motif probably comprising four inward-pointing, heart-shaped leaves with the tesserae laid obliquely to produce serrated divisions between the red, yellow, and white shading; stalks from the base linked each leaf to the *guilloche* circle. Traces of a stepped-triangle occupied the one remaining triangular interspace at the margin. The panel was surrounded by a dark blue-grey triple fillet, which was linked on one corner to a spaced swastika-meander that ran along the western side, and perhaps originally the opposite side. The rectangular space created was filled by a strip of four-strand *guilloche* with broader-than-normal strands of two rows of blue-grey, pale grey, and white except for the central 'bars' executed in red (x2), yellow, and white (an extra one results in a rather clumsy arrangement at one end). Part of the coarse outer border was exposed on the north side, having a red band beside the panel and pale creamy-grey tesserae beyond. Although the size of the mosaic could not be ascertained, the room probably had the same north–south dimension as that with Panel A (5.80 m), in which case Panel C was probably a four-by-four grid of octagons. The workmanship and style confirm that it is contemporary with, and by the same craftsmen as, the neighbouring panel. The saltire arrangement of Panel A is reminiscent of the work of the mid-4th century Saltire Group, seen, for example, on mosaics from Halstock (Dorset) and Tockington Park (Gloucestershire). Although superior in quality, it has the same scheme, including the central poised square, as a mosaic from Dinnington (Somerset) which also has a comparable outer border. The mosaic from Building 13 may thus be attributable to the same group, although its centrepiece is untypical and without parallel in Britain. The design is very occasionally found elsewhere, notably on late mosaics in Spain. However, this, and especially Panel C, have closer affinities with mosaics from Colliton Park in Dorchester, which can be dated to the period after AD 340.

Figure 70: Painting of mosaic from Building 13 Panel B (left) and Panel C (right)

ring-beam footing may explain why the drain caused neither subsidence nor catastrophic collapse of the adjacent walls.

Few finds came from within Building 13 itself or from the area around it and fewer still were both stratified and datable. Whilst clearly belonging to the later Roman period, closer dating of Building 13 has relied on the stylistic aspects of its mosaic floors. These appear to have been integral to its construction and are believed to be consistent with a date in the mid-4th century (Cosh and Neal 2006, 112) although, realistically, this could fall anywhere in the period *c* AD 340–370.

The obsolescence and abandonment of Building 13 is also impossible to date and there is evidence for a change of use late in its existence. Erosion and damage to the mosaic and its bedding mortar clearly took place at a late stage of use and was never repaired. What these new activities were remains unclear. Perhaps they were industrial, but no industrial by-products or residues were recognised and, unlike

Figure 69: Tracing mosaic pattern onto acetate

Figure 71: Lifting the mosaic

Building 12, no ovens were built within it. This damage to the floor could have resulted from agricultural use, possibly even stabling of horses or stalling of livestock. Certainly there was no occupation waste or debris to suggest that the activity was domestic in character. Several patches of scorching were observed in Room 1 and on the *porticus* floor, suggesting that small fires or, perhaps, temporary hearths had been set. A dark loam, rich in fragments of stone, mortar, plaster, and some pottery, sealed the remains of the building and filled the decayed sill-beam trenches.

South of Building 13, a yard or courtyard buried the well-worn middle Roman rubble-surfaced yard beneath more redeposited spreads, which included late 3rd–4th century pottery. These layers were metalled with a layer of crushed Purbeck limestone roof tiles.

West of Building 13, a 4th century ditch was aligned NNE–SSW, cutting through the remains of Building 10 before turning abruptly to the WNW. This is unlikely to be a drainage feature and may, instead, represent an enclosure or boundary. A partial row of late post-holes seems to have been aligned on the south-western corner of Room 1 and may represent an external partition of open land west of Building 13.

Figure 72: Gluing backing to the mosaic prior to lifting

Burials

Several neonates were buried across the site, five graves were found in Building 12 although the remains may represent more than five burials. Two neonates were buried in Room 3 of Building 6 and one came from outside Building 7. Other neonate bones, almost certainly redeposited, came from post-Roman pits cutting the south-west corner of Room 1 in Building 13. As seen elsewhere, the stratigraphic setting of these graves was uncertain, save that they pre-dated the *in situ* demolition deposits. They could have been inserted at any time whilst the building remained standing, and probably illustrate the persistence of this burial rite for at least some very young babies into the 4th century. Six infant burials were found in pits inside a late Roman building at Alington Avenue (Davies *et al.* 2002, 69). Five of these burials were tight up against the south and north walls of the building. At Charles Street infant burials were associated with early and late Roman buildings (Adam *et al.* 1992). At Greyhound Yard the remains of 26 babies aged between 6 months *in utero* to birth were found; only 13 of these came from graves, the remainder were buried in pits, wells, and robber trenches (Rogers 1993, 314–5).

The aisled barn (Building 12)

South of Building 13, on the southern shoulder of the coombe, an aisled barn (Building 12) (Fig. 73) may have been constructed as early as the later 3rd century, although it probably belongs to the first half of the 4th century, and is directly contemporary with Building 13. The eastern wall of this structure was slightly out of alignment with the other three. Two partial rows of large rubble-filled post-pads indicate that substantial internal posts helped to support the roof, and the mortared stone walls may have risen to first storey level at least, for extra strength, and to ensure the security of the building's contents. Part of the eastern wall survived (Fig. 74–75) At the northern end of Building 12, a curious 'dog-legged' ditch (G.711) may have served to drain the exterior of the structure, although the gradient of the feature was to the west, rather than the north, where it could have discharged into the coombe.

Two stone-built ovens (G.720) lay just inside the southern wall of Building 12, where their stratigraphic

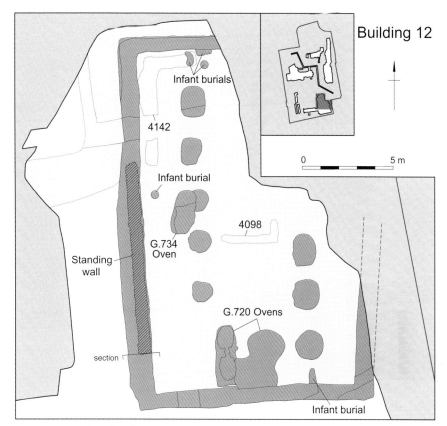

Figure 73: Detailed plan of Building 12

relationship with the building was ambiguous. The eastern oven had been almost entirely destroyed when the south wall of the barn was robbed. It seems likely that these were inserted

at a late stage the use of Building 12 (as seen in the 1969 excavation to the south). A third oven (G.734) lay to the north where it clearly cut the stone packing of a main post-pad. This

Figure 74: Surviving section of masonry walling in Building 12

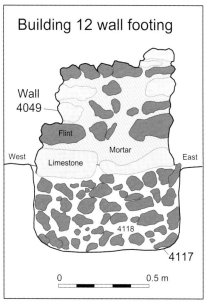

Figure 75: Elevation through Building 12 wall

Figure 76: Reconstruction of a Black Burnished Ware jar

Figure 77: Samian ware and detail of PRISCVS makers stamp

A late Roman finds assemblage

A layer of dark soil (4030) above the *in situ* archaeological deposits of Building 12 contained a particularly rich assemblage of pottery and other finds. Several hundred late 4th century bronze coins, the dispersed remains of a former hoard (see below), were distributed throughout this layer. Other items included a gilded disc brooch, silver and bronze finger-rings, fragments of worked shale and glass vessels, part of a chain, a drill bit and a broken metalworkers' punch made of iron, together with numerous animal bones and marine shells from domestic (cattle, pigs, sheep/goats, horses, dogs, and fowl) and wild (red deer, antler, wigeon, woodcock, oyster, limpet, cockle, and clam) species, as well as abundant ceramic roof tile, brick, limestone, and flint rubble.

Overall, 997 sherds of pottery were recovered, all in good, fresh condition and with an average weight of 23 g. Most were of the very latest Roman date, belonging within the second half of the 4th or even the early 5th century, although a few sherds of South-western Black Burnished ware, late 2nd century samian, other earlier imported table wares and amphorae, together with coins of Hadrian (AD 117–138) and Julia Mammea (AD 222–235; Fig. 78) probably result from the disturbance of earlier deposits beneath. Over 80% of the sherds were from the Wareham/Poole Harbour region, the South-east Dorset Black Burnished ware industry still faithfully supplying the town as it had since the pre-Roman Iron Age. The vessels mainly consisted of shallow circular and, less commonly, oval dishes, flanged bowls and dishes, and jars with everted or flanged rims. It is clear, though, that all was not well within the industry at this time – the surface finishes and decoration afforded to the vessels tended to be more cursory than in preceding periods while unusual inclusions in the clay such as limestone, other rocks, and grog appear in the otherwise sandy fabric, perhaps resulting from the sloppy preparation of clay. Only two new forms were introduced after AD 350 – squat jars/bowls and large storage jars with everted and/or pie-crust rims. These large jars were generally made in coarse, shale-rich, oxidised fabrics and may have been for some new and very specific (perhaps industrial) purpose as they often had small perforations around their necks and sometimes the base too, surrounding a large, central hole made before the pot was fired. A small but still significant proportion of the everted rim jars from this layer and other late groups on the site had been made on a potter's wheel (we cannot be certain whether the bowls were too because the surface treatments applied to them generally mask all traces of manufacturing technique), a technology that the South-east Dorset potters had successfully ignored for the previous 300 years! Sherds from these late groups also indicate that kitchenware from further afield – Devon/south Somerset, South Devon, and the Alice Holt/Farnham area on the Surrey/Hampshire border – were gradually infiltrating the *Durnovarian* markets for the first time. Tablewares (red colour-coated bowls and darker coloured beakers and jugs) and mortaria came exclusively from the Oxfordshire and New Forest pottery industries, while the only imports consisted of a few sherds of North African (Tunisian) cylindrical amphorae, which carried olive oil and, perhaps, fish products from this region.

suggests that the oven was not only later than Building 12 but that the aisled structure had probably lost its roof supports by this time and no longer served anything like its original purpose. Dating the late use of Building 13 remains problematic but sherds from a Black Burnished ware jar (Fig. 76) from the backfill of oven G.734 are significant; vessels of this type are believed to have been produced only after AD 350, possibly continuing into the earlier 5th century (Seager Smith and Davies 1993, 233).

Figure 78: Coin of Julia Mamaea, dia. 28 mm

Among the most significant discoveries from the Hascombe Court excavations were the scattered remains of a late 4th or early 5th century coin hoard (Fig. 79). It is not now possible to say exactly how large the hoard originally was but it probably included most of the 409 copper alloy coins found inside Building 12. This group included earlier 4th century coins and even some radiates from the later 3rd century, but was dominated by small *nummii* of the House of Theodosius, dating between AD 388 and 402. After closure of the mint at London in AD 326, Britain again became dependant on continental sources for its monetary supply. The issues of Honorius and Arcadius within the hoard represent the last bulk issues of small denomination bronze coinage to reach the shores of Roman Britain.

Of the coins from Building 12, most came from a single layer of rubbly dark soil (layer 4030) overlying *in situ* deposits. A smaller number of coins had intruded into earlier deposits, primarily by the action of earthworms, small burrowing animals, and plant-roots moving the coins downwards. The hoard was probably originally concealed within the superstructure of Building 12, being scattered as this disintegrated. Coins were most densely clustered in the northern part of the building but this was probably because layer 4030 survived most deeply in this area. The date at which the hoard was assembled remains unclear, but its closure is unlikely to pre-date the turn of the 5th century and wear on some of the coins suggests it may have been any time within the first two to three decades of that century.

In 1969 a similar late hoard was found immediately to the south also within the late and post-abandonment soils overlying parts of a range of 4th century building (Patrick Greene 1993). Detailed analysis indicateed that the two groups of coins represent separate, distinct hoards, with that from Hascombe Court possibly being assembled at a slightly later date (Cooke 2007).

Figure 79: Selected coins from the hoard including Honorius (left), dia. up to 14 mm

Late Roman features south of Building 12

In the open area south of Building 12, north of Patrick Greene's Building 1, several features were associated with the agricultural/industrial complex (Fig. 57). The vestigial remnants of early Roman boundary ditch G.739 probably became fully infilled at this time. Three pits (G.707) were investigated. One of these was only 0.5 m deep, but the other two were vertically-sided, subrectangular 'shaft pits' of a type previously recognised in Dorchester on sites such as Greyhound Yard (Woodward *et al.* 1993, 48, 51) and County Hall (Smith 1993, 15). One exceeded 1.6 m deep and was not excavated below this depth; the other (immediately to the south-west) was mechanically excavated to 2.8 m without reaching its base. Amongst the finds from one of these pits were substantial parts of a small Dressel 20, or possibly Dressel 23, amphora, made in the Spanish province of Baetica and almost certainly old when it was deposited. A post-firing graffiti scratched into its rim was too worn and chipped to be legible, but a maker's stamp reading LQS (cf., Callender 1965, 164, fig. 9, 34–9; Remesal Rodriguez 1986, 187–9 and 254, no. 216) is an abbreviation of *L. Quintus Secundus* and is generally dated to the 2nd century. Other sherds from this amphora came from the upper infill of ditch G.739. The uppermost fill of the same pit also contained bones from the right hind leg of an adult pony (estimated at 1.28 m or 13 hands at the withers). No evidence for gnawing was noted on the bones and no butchery marks were found but their occurrence may indicate disposal of unwanted parts after the animal was slaughtered. A metatarsus, probably from a second horse, showed bone pathology consistent with use as a draught animal. Single bones of duck/mallard, carrion crow, and a juvenile long-eared owl were also found in the same pit. Bones from small marine and freshwater fish, small birds, a shrew, and many tiny fragments of large mammal bones were found in the lower deposits. Dog coprolites are a likely source for some of these bone fragments while much of the rest, and perhaps the fish, is likely to have come from cess deposits, further indicated by the presence of cess fly pupae. Mineralised plant remains include sloes (*Prunus spinosa*) and apple pips (*Malus*), which are also likely to have come from human consumption (either having been spat out or passed through).

A short, vertically-sided ditch (G.742) was dug. This measured 1.85 m wide by at least 5 m long and in excess of 1.4 m deep and was possibly a latrine. It was of probable 4th century date but was infilled before pit 4268 was dug. Within the probable latrine were numerous thin layers of silt and loam that had slumped very markedly as it became infilled. Among these layers were lenses that contained very small fish remains of a similar nature to the deposit in oven 1356. Most of the remains were of very small whole herrings and this deposit was, again, likely to be of *allec*. The southern end of this feature may have been among those seen in the 1969 excavation immediately to the south (Patrick Greene 1993, 74), giving the trench a full length of *c* 6 m. Just to the south there was a small undated oven.

Evidence for latest 3rd and 4th century activity was mainly confined to the Somerleigh Court Nursing Home and Hascombe Court excavations. Street-front buildings of moderate to high status were present up until the later 3rd century, after which a period of decline and/or alternative usage can

Figure 80: Pits cutting the mosaic in Building 13

be inferred from the damage to the mosaic floor in Building 6 and, possibly, from the crude unmortared tessellated floor inserted into Building 14, both of which were sealed by layers containing coins of Carausius (AD 286–293) and Allectus (AD 293–296). There is little, if any, evidence that the structures survived.

Understanding of late Roman urban farmsteads is currently in its early stages: future research excavations might address more closely the implications that such establishments may have for towns in terms of economy, of the range of activities carried out, and of the relationship, not only between the high status houses and their ancillary buildings within town walls, but also between the intra-mural site and what must be assumed to be its far more extensive rural landholdings. It may be that such establishments bear at least superficial comparison with medieval manors and their associated home farms, rather than with earlier Roman urban settlements.

Two other late Roman farmsteads have previously been proposed within Dorchester, at Colliton Park and Greyhound Yard (Woodward *et al.* 1993, 369), both of which saw construction of later Roman aisled barns near wealthier domestic buildings. Further afield, urban farmsteads can be cited in Cirencester, St Albans (Wacher 1974), Winchester (where, in some places, dark earths were forming over formerly urban land in the late Roman period), and London (Reece 1980; Marsden 1985). This is not to say that crops or livestock were necessarily being farmed on an intensive or systematic basis inside the town although dark, midden-based soils had evidently started to accumulate in some parts of Dorchester in the late Roman period (Woodward 1993, 371–2). At Greyhound Yard, evidence was found for an arable soil horizon sealed below post-Roman 'dark earth' layers (Staines 1993, 314). It has also been suggested that some animal husbandry, most notably pig-breeding, took place within, rather than around, *Durnovaria*. There seems to be little tradition of pig-rearing around the town, but considerable evidence for consumption within it (Maltby 1993, 326; Woodward 1993, 372).

Later activity

A full history of post-Roman Dorchester lies beyond the scope of this book; only the slightest evidence for 5th century activity came from the excavations (namely the dispersed late coin hoard, concentrations of late Roman pottery in reworked soil layers around Building 12, and a cluster of pits (G.612, Fig. 80–81) cutting the south-west corner of Room 1 in Building 13). It might be reasonable to suppose that settlement, agricultural and industrial activity persisted within the town walls into the second, perhaps even the third, decade of the 5th century but there is no evidence that this preserved anything of the town's 2nd and 3rd century urban character.

Whatever remained of Roman towns in Britain fell into disuse during the early-mid 5th century. No central government remained to underwrite their upkeep, nor were they now necessary (Reece 1980, 88). The economic, industrial and social circumstances which called towns (rather than hamlets or villages) into existence did not arise again in Britain until the later 7th century, which saw the growth of Middle Saxon trading emporia such as *Hamwic*, precursor of Southampton (Andrews *et al.* 2005, 195).

Post-Roman settlement has been found outside Roman Dorchester, immediately east of Poundbury hillfort. Here structures that post-dated abandonment of the late Roman cemetery (Sparey Green 1987) have been linked with a period of occupation and refortification of the hillfort (Ellison 1987, 14–15). Also possibly of late Roman or sub-Roman date are rectangular timber buildings found at Alington Avenue (Davies *et al.* 2002, 171–9).

Figure 81: Late Roman/post-Roman erosion to former mosaic floor, Building 13

The growth of medieval and post-medieval Dorchester had little direct impact upon the site, other than through its sporadic exploitation as a ready source of building stone. Many irregular trenches and hollows attest considerable effort in grubbing-out Roman masonry for re-use in later periods. A silver half-penny of Henry V

Figure 82: Coin of Henry V, dia. 14 mm

(1413–1422, Fig. 82) came from the dark garden soils of Chesil Place and only a small assemblage of medieval and post-medieval pottery (138 sherds) was recovered from the 2000–1 excavations. Most of the town wall was probably destroyed before the 17th century. A boundary claim by the manor of Fordington in 1607 partly followed '*the Topp or Crest of the banckes called the Walles which doe circuit and bounde in the towne and groundes of the town of Dorchester*' but was able to make specific reference to '*a peece of Wall on the southside of West Yate*' (gate). Other parts of the wall also probably survived at this time (RCHM(E) 1970, 542–3) but, with the single exception of a short segment extant in Albert Road, all are now gone.

Hascombe Court

Acknowledgements

The programme of excavations undertaken at the former County Hospital site during 2000–1 was funded by the site's developer, Bentleigh Cross Ltd. In particular Wessex Archaeology would like thank Tony Murley, Robin Waterer, and Geoff Strong for their support and assistance throughout the project. CgMs Consulting Ltd acted as consultants and the preliminary research, project management, and assistance of Angus Stephenson and Rob Bourne is gratefully acknowledged. Thanks are also extended to Steve Wallis (Senior Archaeologist, Dorset County Council) who monitored the progress of the project on behalf of the local planning authority. Andrew Martin, (Principal Planning Officer, West Dorset District Council) is thanked for his support during the project.

The fieldwork was managed for Wessex Archaeology by Jonathan Nowell and directed by Mike Trevarthen, assisted by Jo Best, Paul Pearce, and Mike Dinwiddy. The excavation team comprised Dominic Barker, Jeff Braithwaite, Gareth Chaffey, Jon Crisp, Paul Gajos, Chris Heatley, Guy Kendall, Stephen Legg, Grace Jones, Hannah Marriot, Faye Minter, Kate O'Farrell, Pauline Phillips, Nick Plunkett, Andrea Proffitt, Steve Tatler, Gareth Thomas, Ciorstaidh Hayward Trevarthen, Gary Wickenden, and Nicholas Winskill. Plant and operators were provided by G. Crooke & Sons (Dorchester) and Wessex Archaeology is also grateful to Stansells Limited for their on-site co-operation and logistical assistance.

The Somerleigh Court Nursing Home mosaic pavements were recorded by Stephen R. Cosh (ASPROM). Conservation and lifting of the mosaics was undertaken by Virginia Neal assisted on site by Steve Tatler and Faye Minter.

We are grateful to Stephen R. Cosh and David Neal for permission to reproduce Figures 64, 68 and 70. Co-ordination of finds processing and data entry were undertaken by Rachael Seager Smith and Jan Symmonds. Caroline Budd digitised the site plans.

Wessex Archaeology wish to thank members of the Weymouth and Portland Metal Detecting Club, the Stour Valley Search and Recovery Club and the Yeovil and District Bottle Collecting and Metal Detecting Club who gave their time to assist with controlled searching of the site, in particular Colin Bell, Dave Cobb, Margaret Hamilton, John House, Anne Laverty, Robert Lovett, Jean Lovett, Mike Pittard, Paul Rainford, Martin Savage, Martin Thorpe, and Alan Worth. Club liaison was facilitated by Ciorstaidh Hayward Trevarthen, Somerset and Dorset Finds Liaison Officer, Portable Antiquities Scheme.

The post-excavation and publication programme was managed by Bruno Barber, Karen Walker, and Philippa Bradley. Lorraine Mepham managed the finds processing and archive preparation and Michael J. Allen the environmental programme. The finds and environmental specialists are thanked for their contributions to this report and to the initial assessment. Bob Hill, Rob Perrin and Bob Davis provided useful comment on structural aspects of the late Roman town house and individual artefacts. Karen Walker, Susan M. Davies, Rachael Seager Smith, Roland Smith, and Steve Wallis commented helpfully on an earlier version of the text. The report was edited by Philippa Bradley and Julie Gardiner. Illustrations, design and typesetting are by Karen Nichols. Artefact photographs were taken by Elaine A. Wakefield, the photograph of Maiden Castle (Fig. 8) is by John Vallender and the fish bones is by Sheila Hamilton-Dyer (Fig. 24). The archive was prepared for deposition by Christine Butterworth.

Information from the Dorset Sites and Monuments Record was supplied by Claire Pinder and data from the Dorchester Urban Archaeological Database was provided by Peter Bellamy. Additional information on the site's developmental history and on other unpublished local archaeological observations was provided by Christopher Sparey Green, David Ashford, and Peter Woodward. Staff at the Dorset County Record Office are thanked for their help with background research. Fraser Donachie, Michael A. Hodges, and Ian Messer of the Christchurch Local History Society are thanked for their help with supplying the image of Benjamin Ferrey (Fig. 4), which is reproduced with kind permission of the Society. Mark Forrest, Dorset History Centre is thanked for permission to reproduce Benjamin Ferrey's drawing of the proposed County Hospital Fig. 5 (reference number NG/HH/DO(C)/6/1). Geoff Strong (Bentleigh Cross Ltd) kindly supplied photographs of the development (Figs 3, 83). It is anticipated that the archive will be deposited with Dorset County Museum; it is currently held at Wessex Archaeology under the project codes 48784 (excavation) and 56530 (post-excavation).

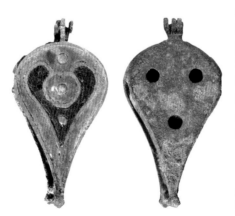

Roman seal matrix box with enamelled decoration, length 46 mm

Bibliography

Adam, NJ & Butterworth, CA, 1993, Excavations at Wessex Court, Charles Street, Dorchester, Dorset 1990, unpub, Wessex Archaeology, rep ref 33721

Adam, NJ, Butterworth, CA, Davies, SM & Farwell, DE, 1992, Excavations at Wessex Court, Charles Street, Dorchester, Dorset 1989, unpub, Wessex Archaeology, rep ref 32812

Aitken, G & Aitken, N, 1982, Excavations on the Library site, Colliton Park, Dorchester, 1961–3, *Proc Dorset Natur Hist Archaeol Soc* **104**, 93–126

Andrews, P, Birbeck, V & Stoodley, N, 2005, Concluding discussion, in V Birbeck, , RJC Smith, P Andrews & N Stoodley, *The Origins of Mid-Saxon Southampton: Excavations at the Friends Provident St.Mary's Stadium 1998–2000*. Salisbury, Wessex Archaeology, 190–204

Attwooll, M, undated, Black Wednesday, 1897, http:/dorsetlife.co.uk/articles/ArticlesDetail.asp?ID=544

Bateman N & Locker A, 1982, The sauce of the Thames, *London Archaeol*, **4**(**8**), 204–7

Barnes, I, 1997, Part 3: A37 Western Link Road, 5, Fordington Bottom: site description, in Smith *et al.* 1997, 203–21

Bellamy, PS, 2004, Roman defences at Dorford Baptist Church, Bridport Road, Dorchester, *Proc Dorset Natur Hist & Archaeol Soc* **126**, 166–70

Bidwell, PT, 1979, *The Legionary Bath-House and Basilica and Forum at Exeter*. Exeter, Exeter Archaeol Rep **1**

Boon, GC, 1988, Counterfeit coins in Roman Britain, in J Casey & R Reece (eds), *Coins and the Archaeologist*, 2nd edn, London, Seaby, 102–88

Bradley, R, 1975, *Maumbury Rings, Dorchester: the excavations of 1908–1913*. London, Society of Antiquaries

Burnham, BC & Wacher, J, 1990, *The 'Small Towns' of Roman Britain*, London, Batsford

Callender, MH, 1965, *Roman Amphorae with Index of Stamps*, London, Oxford University Press

Celsus, *On Medicine*, Loeb Classical Library (trans. WG Spencer 1935)

Cooke, N, 2007, A late Roman coin hoard from the County Hospital site, Dorchester, *Proc Dorset Natur Hist Archaeol Soc* **128**, 61–7

Cosh, SR & Neal, DS, 2006, *Roman Mosaics of Britain: Volume II: South-West Britain*. London, Society of Antiquaries

Cunliffe, B, 1974, *Iron Age Communities in Britain: an account of England, Scotland and Wales from the seventh century BC until the Roman Conquest*, London, Book Club Associates

Curtis, RI, 1991, *Garum and Salsamenta. Production and Commerce in Material Medica*, Leiden, Brill

Davies, SM, Bellamy, P, Heaton, MJ & Woodward, PJ, 2002, *Excavations at Alington Avenue, Fordington, Dorchester, Dorset 1984–87*, Dorchester, Dorset Natur Hist Archaeol Soc Monogr **15**

Dobney, KM, Jaques S.D, & Irving BG, 1996, Of butchers and breeds, Rep on vertebrate remains from various sites in the City of Lincoln, Lincoln, *Lincoln Archaeological Studies* **5**

Draper, J, 1992, *Dorchester An Illustrated History*, Wimborne, Dovecote Press

Draper, J & Chaplin, C, 1982, *Dorchester Excavations Volume 1*. Dorset Natur Hist Archaeol Soc Monogr **2**

Drew, CD & Collingwood, KCS, 1937, First interim report on the excavations at Colliton Park, Dorchester, 1937–1938, *Proc Dorset Natur Hist Archaeol Soc* **59**,

Drew, CD, and Collingwood, KCS, 1938, The excavations at Colliton Park, Dorchester; second interim rep, *Proc Dorset Natur Hist Archaeol Soc* **60**, 51–65

Esmonde Cleary, S, 1987, *Extra-Mural Areas of Romano-British Towns*. Oxford, British Archaeol Rep **169**

Esmonde Cleary, EA, 1989, *The Ending of Roman Britain*. London, Batsford

Ellison, A, 1987, Phase summary, in Sparey Green 1987, 14–15

Farwell, DE & Molleson, TI, 1993, *Excavations at Poundbury 1966-88 Volume 2: the cemeteries*. Dorchester, Dorset Natur Hist Archaeol Soc Monogr **11**

Field, NH, 1992 *Dorset and the Second Legion: new light on a Roman campaign*, Tiverton, Dorset Books

Foster E, 1768, *An Essay on Hospitals. Or, Succinct Directions for the Situation, Construction and Administration of Country Hospitals*, Dublin

Frere, S, 1974, *Britannia: a history of Roman Britain*, London, Book Club Associates

Hinton, DA, 1998, *Saxons & Vikings*. Wimborne, Dovecote Press

Hulka, S & Hodgson, J, 2000, Dorchester old county hospital, in Dorset Archaeology in 2000, *Proc Dorset Natur Hist Archaeol Soc* **122**, 162

Ireland, S, 1988, *Roman Britain: a sourcebook*. London, Routledge

Johnson, S, 1986, *Later Roman Britain*, London, Paladin Grafton

Leach, P, 2001, *Roman Somerset*. Wimborne, Dovecote Press

Maltby, M, 1993, Animal bones, in Woodward *et al.* 1993, 315–40

Marsden, P, 1985, London in the 3rd and 4th centuries, in F Grew & B Hobley, *Roman Urban Topography in Britain and the Western Empire*, London, CBA Res Rep **59**, 99–108

Millett, M, 1992, *The Romanisation of Britain: an essay in archaeological interpretation*, Cambridge, Cambridge University Press

Moule, HJ, 1906, *Dorchester Antiquities* (2nd edn), Dorchester, Henry Ling

O'Connor, TP, 1988, *Bones from the General Accident Site, Tanner Row*, York, Archaeology of York Fascicule **15.2**

Neer, van, W & Lentacker, A, 1994, New archaeozoological evidence for the consumption of locally-produced fish sauce in the northern provinces of the Roman empire, *Archaeofauna* **3**, 53–62

Newman, J & Pevsner N, 1972. *The Buildings of England. Dorset,* Harmondsworth, Penguin

Patrick Greene, J, 1993, Excavations at Dorchester Hospital (Site C), Dorchester, Dorset, *Proc Dorset Natur Hist Archaeol Soc* **115**, 71–101

Peddie, J, 1997, *Conquest: the Roman invasion of Britain*, Stroud, Sutton

Penn, KJ, 1980, *Historic Towns in Dorset*. Dorchester, Dorset Natur Hist Archaeol Soc Monogr **1**

Philpott, R, 1991, *Burial Practices in Roman Britain: a survey of grave treatment and furnishing AD 43–410*. Oxford, British Archaeol Rep **219**

Pliny, *Natural History*, Loeb Classical Library (trans by H. Rackham 1938)

Putnam, WG, 1998, Dorchester Roman aqueduct 1998, *Proc Dorset Natur Hist Archaeol Soc* **120**, 94–6

Putnam, W, undated, *The Roman Town House at Dorchester*. Dorchester, Dorset County Council

Royal Commission on Historical Monuments (England) 1970, *An Inventory of Historical Monuments in the County of Dorset: Volume Two South-East (Part 3)*. London, HMSO

Reece, R, 1980, Town and country: the end of Roman Britain, *World Archaeology* **12**(**1**), 11–20

Reece, R, 1993, Roman coins, in Woodward *et al.* 1993, 114–16

Rivet, ALF, 1970a, *Town and Country in Roman Britain*, London, Hutchinson University Library

Rivet, ALF, 1970b, The British section of the Antonine Itinerary, *Britannia* **1**, 34–82

Remesal Rodriguez, J, 1986, *La Annona Militaris y la Exportacion de Aceite Betico a Germania*, Madrid

Rogers, J, 1993, The human remains, in Woodward *et al.* 1993, 314–5

Seager Smith, R & Davies, SM, 1993, Roman Pottery, in Woodward *et al.* 1993, 202–14

Smith, RJC, 1993, *Excavations at County Hall, Dorchester, Dorset, 1988, in the North-West Quarter of Durnovaria*, Salisbury, Wessex Archaeology Rep **4**

Sparey Green, C 1987, *Excavations at Poundbury, Dorchester, Dorset, 1966–1982, Vol. I: the settlements*, Dorchester, Dorset Natur Hist Archaeol Soc Monogr 7

Staines, S, 1993, The soils, in Woodward *et al.* 1993, 313–14

Stephenson, A, 1998, Archaeological Impact Assessment: Dorset County Hospital Site, Princes Street, Dorchester. Unpub client rep, CgMs Consulting, document reference AS/KB/2367

Stevenson C, 2000, *Medicine and Magnificence British Hospital and Asylum Architecture 1660–1815*, Yale University Press

Straker, V, 1984, First and second century carbonised cereal grain from Roman London, in W van Zeist & WA Casparie (eds), *Plants and Ancient Man: studies in palaeoethnobotany*, Rotterdam, A A Balkema, 323–29

Tomlin, RSO, 1993, Graffiti on pottery, in Woodward *et al.* 1993, 284–5

Wacher, JS, 1974, Villae in urbibus, *Britannia* **5**, 282–4

Wacher, J, 1978, *The Towns of Roman Britain*. London, Book Club Associates

Wessex Archaeology, 1994, Watching Brief at the site of the Forum Centre, Trinity Street, Dorchester, unpub client rep, ref 37111

Wessex Archaeology, 2005, Dorchester Post Office Site, Dorchester, Dorset, unpub client rep, ref 60970

Wessex Archaeology, 2007a, Land North of Poundbury Farm, Poundbury, Dorchester, Dorset: Archaeological Evaluation, unpub client rep, ref 60021.02

Wessex Archaeology, 2007b, Little Keep, Dorchester, Dorset. Post-excavation assessment report and updated project design for analysis and publication, unpub client rep, ref 64912.02

Wilson, D, 1971, Roman Britain in 1970: Southern Counties, *Britannia* **2**, 279

Woodward, PJ, 1993, Discussion, in Woodward *et al.* 1993, 351–82

Woodward, PJ, Davies, SM & Hunt, AH, 1993, *Excavations at the Old Methodist Chapel and Greyhound Yard, Dorchester*, 1981–1984, Dorset Natur Hist Archaeol Soc Monogr **12**

http://www.romans-in-britain.org.uk/arl_roman_recipes-garum_fish_sauce.htm

http://www.penelope.uchicago.edu/~grout/encyclopaedia_romana/wine/garum.html

http://www.medicinaantiqua.org.uk/bio_gal.html

http://www.unrv.com/culture/roman-medicine.php

http://penelope.uchicago.edu~grout/encyclopaedia_romana/wine/apicius.html

Coin of Vespasian, dia. 26 mm

Internet Reports

Index of Specialist Reports

http://www.wessexarch.co.uk/projects/dorset/dorchester_hospital/

Gilt boss brooch, dia. 21 mm